Study Guide for Damodaran on Valuation

WILEY PROFESSIONAL BANKING AND FINANCE SERIES

EDWARD I. ALTMAN, Editor

Study Guide for
Damodaran on Valuation

Security Analysis for Investment and Corporate Finance

Aswath Damodaran

John Wiley & Sons, Inc.
New York • Brisbane • Chichester • Singapore • Toronto

This paper is printed on acid free paper.

Copyright ©1994 by Aswath Damodaran
Published by John Wiley & Sons, Inc.

All rights reserved. Published simultaneously in Canada.

Library of Congress Cataloging in Publication Data:

Damodaran, Aswath
    Study guide for Damodaran on valuation/ Aswath Damodaran.
    p.   cm.
  Includes bibliographical references and index
  ISBN 0-471-30465-4 (cloth).--ISBN 0-471-01450-8 (book/disk)
    ISBN 0-471-10897-9 (paper)
  1. Corporations--Valuation--Mathematical models. 2. Capital asset
pricing model. I. Title. II. Title: On valuation
  HG4028.V3D35 1994
658.15--dc20   93-21405

Printed in the United States of America

10 9 8 7 6 5 4 3 2 1

ACKNOWLEDGEMENTS

I would like to thank the students in the Equity Valuation class I taught in the Spring of 1994 at the Stern School of Business, who worked through many of the problems in this book and gave me useful feedback on the same. I would also like to thank Jacqueline Urinyi at John Wiley, whose patience and guidance helped me put the manuscript together. Any errors or omissions are my own.

PREFACE

This study guide is designed to supplement my book *Damodaran on Valuation (Wiley 1994)*, and the problems and solutions in each chapter build on the same chapter in the book.

The valuation models described in *Damodaran on Valuation* are fairly straightforward, but the only way to learn how to use valuation models is to practice on real world examples. This book provides a number of exercises, based upon real companies, for each of the models described in the book. Some of these problems require significant computations, and the use of a computer spreadsheet is recommended, though not necessary. The solutions to the exercises are at the end of the book.

In working through these exercises, I would recommend that the reader, in addition to working through the numbers, also attempt to understand the concepts underlying the models.

TABLE OF CONTENTS

Questions

Solutions

CHAPTER 1

INTRODUCTION TO VALUATION

This chapter provides the philosophical basis for the valuation models used in this book. It examines the uses of valuation in a number of settings - portfolio management, mergers and acquisitions and corporate finance. It also relates the use of valuation methods to investment philosophies.

Question 1 - Valuation Philosophy
There are many who claim that value is based upon investor perceptions, and perceptions alone, and that cash flows and earnings do not matter. This argument is flawed because

A. value is determined by earnings and cash flows, and investor perceptions do not matter.

B. perceptions do matter, but they can change. Value must be based upon something more stable.

C. investors are irrational. Therefore, their perceptions should not determine value.

D. value is determined by investor perceptions, but it is also determined by the underlying earnings and cash flows. Perceptions must be based upon reality.

Question 2 - Valuation and Efficiency
You use a valuation model to arrive at a value of $15 for a stock. The market price of the stock is $25. The difference can be explained by

A. a market inefficiency; the market is overvaluing the stock.

B. the use of the wrong valuation model to value the stock.

C. errors in the inputs to the valuation model.

D. none of the above

E. either A, B, or C.

Question 3 - Valuation Propositions

Valuation is based upon quantitative factors. It does not take into account qualitative factors such as the quality of management or brand name value. Is this statement true or false?

Question 4 - Bias in Valuation

There is no such thing as an unbiased valuation. Since the biases of the analyst affect any valuation done by him or her, valuation is worthless. Is this statement true or false?

Question 5 - Valuation and New Information

If no new information comes out about a firm, there is no need to update any valuation done on that firm. Is this statement true or false?

Question 6 - Valuation and Uncertainty

You value two firms. You obtain a fairly precise estimate of value for Firm A, but you arrive at a much more imprecise estimate of value for Firm B. You must have done a better job valuing the former. Is this statement true or false?

Question 7 - Valuation and Complexity

You have to choose between two valuation models. One model is a very simple model with few inputs. The other is a much more realistic model that requires several more inputs. Which one will provide the better valuation and why?

Question 8 - Valuation and Efficient Markets

"If you are a believer in market efficiency, there is no point in doing valuation." Is this statement true or false?

Question 9 - Valuation and Fundamental Analysis

A portfolio manager uses the dividend discount model to value stocks, buys stocks that come out as undervalued in the model, and sells stocks that come out as overvalued. What are the conditions under which you would expect this portfolio manager to be successful?

Question 10 - Valuation and Industry Background

Assume that you are an equity research analyst following the retail sector. How would a prior background in retailing (assume that you used to be a manager at a major department store before you became an equity research analyst) help you in your new job?

Question 11 - Valuation and Charting

Technical analysis (charting) and valuation are alternative approaches to investing, and are fundamentally incompatible. Is this statement true or false?

Question 12 - Valuation and Trading

You are an equity trader, who takes short-term positions on stocks, prior to the release of new information (such as earnings or dividend announcements). Valuation models, you believe, are based upon long time horizons. Is there a role for valuation models in your trading?

4 Questions

Question 13 - Valuation and Takeovers
You cannot use valuation models in takeovers, since takeovers usually encompass factors that cannot be valued -- such as synergy and strategic considerations. Is this statement true or false?

Question 14 - Valuation and Public Relations
The value of a firm is determined by the market. If management wants to increase value, it has to be good at public relations and should maintain good relationships with its analysts. Will this be sufficient?

CHAPTER 2

APPROACHES TO VALUATION

Analysts use a wide range of models in practice, ranging from the simple to the sophisticated. These models often make very different assumptions about pricing, but they do share some common characteristics and can be classified in broader terms. There are several advantages to such a classification -- it is easier to understand where individual models fit in to the big picture, why they provide different results, and when they have fundamental errors in logic.

Question 1 - DCF Valuation Fundamentals

Discounted cash flow valuation is based upon the notion that the value of an asset is the present value of the expected cash flows on that asset, discounted at a rate that reflects the riskiness of those cash flows. Specify whether the following statements about discounted cash flow valuation are true or false, assuming that all variables are constant except for the variable discussed below:

A. As the discount rate increases, the value of an asset increases.

B. As the expected growth rate in cash flows increases, the value of an asset increases.

C. As the life of an asset is lengthened, the value of that asset increases.

D. As the uncertainty about the expected cash flows increases, the value of an asset increases.

E. An asset with an infinite life (i.e., it is expected to last forever) will have an infinite value.

6 Questions

Question 2 - Approaches to DCF Valuation

There are two approaches to valuation. The first approach is to value the equity in the firm. The second approach is to value the entire firm. What is the distinction? Why does it matter?

Question 3 - Mismatching Cash flows and Discount Rates

The following are the projected cash flows to equity and to the firm over the next five years:

Year	CF to Equity	Int (1-t)	CF to Firm
1	$250.00	$90.00	$340.00
2	$262.50	$94.50	$357.00
3	$275.63	$99.23	$374.85
4	$289.41	$104.19	$393.59
5	$303.88	$109.40	$413.27
Terminal Value	$3,946.50		$6,000.00

(The terminal value is the value of the equity or firm at the end of year 5.) The firm has a cost of equity of 12% and a cost of capital of 9.94%. Answer the following questions:

   A. What is the value of the equity in this firm?

   B. What is the value of the firm?

Question 4 - Problems in DCF Valuation

Why might discounted cash flow valuation be difficult to do for the following types of firms?

   A. A private firm, where the owner is planning to sell the firm.

   B. A biotechnology firm, with no current products or sales, but with several promising product patents in the pipeline.

   C. A cyclical firm, during a recession.

D. A troubled firm, which has made significant losses and is not expected to get out of trouble for a few years.

E. A firm, which is in the process of restructuring, where it is selling some of its assets and changing its financial mix.

F. A firm, which owns a lot of valuable land that is currently unutilized.

Question 5 - Relative Valuation: Fundamentals

An analyst tells you that he uses price/earnings multiples, rather than discounted cash flow valuation, to value stocks, because he does not like making assumptions about fundamentals - growth, risk, and payout ratios. Is his reasoning correct?

Question 6 - Industry Average P/E Ratios

You are estimating the price/earnings multiple to use to value Paramount Corporation, by looking at the average price/earnings multiple of comparable firms. The following are the price/earnings ratios of firms in the entertainment business.

Firm	P/E Ratio
Disney (Walt)	22.09
Time Warner	36.00
King World Productions	14.10
New Line Cinema	26.70
CCL	19.12
PLG	23.33
CIR	22.91
GET	97.60
GTK	26.00

A. What is the average P/E ratio?

B. Would you use all the comparable firms in calculating the average? Why or why not?

C. What assumptions are you making when you use the industry-average P/E ratio to value Paramount Communications?

CHAPTER 3

ESTIMATION OF DISCOUNT RATES

The discount rate is a critical ingredient in discounted cash flow valuation. Errors in estimating the discount rate or mismatching cash flows and discount rates can lead to serious errors in valuation. At an intuitive level, the discount rate used should be consistent with both the riskiness and the type of cash flow being discounted. Though there is no consensus among practitioners on the right model to use for measuring risk, there is agreement that higher-risk cash flows should be discounted at a higher rate.

This chapter examines the process of estimating discount rates -- the cost of equity to be used in discounting cash flows to equity, and the cost of capital to be used in discounting cash flows to the firm.

Question 1 - CAPM: Historical Risk Premiums

The following table summarizes risk premiums for stocks in the United States, relative to treasury bills and bonds, for different time periods:

Magnitude of the Risk Premium

Historical Period	Stocks - T.Bills		Stocks - T.Bonds	
	Arithmetic	Geometric	Arithmetic	Geometric
1926-1990	8.41%	6.41%	7.24%	5.50%
1962-1990	4.10%	2.95%	3.92%	3.25%
1981-1990	6.05%	5.38%	0.13%	0.19%

A. What does this premium measure?

B. Why is the geometric mean lower than the arithmetic mean for both bonds and bills?

C. If you had to use a risk premium, would you use the most recent data (1981-1990), or would you use the longer periods? Explain your reasoning.

Question 2 - CAPM: Premiums in Emerging Markets

You are an investor who is interested in the emerging markets of Asia. You are trying to value some stocks in Malaysia, which does not have a long history of financial markets. During the last two years, the stock market has gone up 60% a year, while the government borrowing rate has been 15%, yielding an historical premium of 45%. Would you use this as your risk premium, looking into the future? If not, what would you base your estimate of the premium on?

Question 3 - Using the CAPM

The beta for Eastman Kodak is 1.10. The current six-month treasury bill rate is 3.25%, while the thirty-year bond rate is 6.25%. Estimate the cost of equity for Eastman Kodak, based upon

  (a) using the treasury bill rate as your risk-free rate.
  (b) using the treasury bond rate as your risk-free rate.

(Use the premiums in the table in question 1, if necessary.)

Which one of these estimates would you use in valuation? Why?

Question 4 - Estimating CAPM parameters

You are trying to estimate the cost of equity to use in valuing Daimler Benz, and a data service reports a beta estimate of 0.90. However, the beta is estimated relative to the Frankfurt Stock Exchange (DAX). If you were an international portfolio manager with holdings across many markets, would you use this beta estimate? How would you estimate beta to meet your needs?

Question 5 - CAPM: Divisional and Corporate Betas

You have been asked to estimate the beta of a high-technology firm which has three divisions with the following characteristics

Division	Beta	Market Value
Personal Computers	1.60	$100 million
Software	2.00	$150 million
Computer Mainframes	1.20	$250 million

A. What is the beta of the equity of the firm?

B. What would happen to the beta of equity if the firm divested itself of its software business?

C. If you were asked to value the software business for the divestiture, which beta would you use in your valuation?

Question 6 - CAPM: Betas and Financial Leverage

The following are the betas of the equity of four forestry/paper product companies, and their debt/equity ratios.

Company	Beta	Debt/Equity Ratio
Weyerhauser	1.15	33.91%
Champion International	1.18	54.14%
Intenational Paper	1.05	45.50%
Kimberly-Clark	0.91	11.29%

(All the firms face a corporate tax rate of 40%)

A. Estimate the unlevered beta of each firm. What do the unlevered betas tell you about these firms?

B. Assume now that Kimberly Clark is planning to increase its debt/equity ratio to 30%. What will its new beta be?

C. If you were valuing an initial public offering in the paper products area, what beta would you use in the valuation? (Assume that the firm going public plans to have a debt/equity ratio of 40%.)

Question 7 - Betas and Operating Leverage

The following is a description of the cost structure and betas of five firms in the food production industry:

Company	Fixed Costs	Variable Costs	Beta	D/(D+E)
CPC International	62%	38%	1.23	18.83%
Ralston Purina	47%	53%	0.81	38.32%
Quaker Oats	45%	55%	0.75	13.28%
Chiquita	50%	50%	0.88	75.35%
Kellogg's	40%	60%	0.76	5.57%

(Assume that all firms have a tax rate of 40%.)

A. Based upon just the operating leverage, which firms would you expect to have the highest and lowest betas (assuming that they are in the same business)?

B. Chiquita's beta is believed to be misleading because its financial leverage has increased dramatically since the period when the beta was estimated. If the average D/(D+E) ratio during the period of the regression (to estimate the betas) was only 30%, what would your new estimate of Chiquita's beta be?

Question 8 - CAPM: Betas and Private Firms

You are attempting to estimate the beta of a private firm that has no comparable firms. You decide to estimate an "accounting" beta using past earnings. You have six years of accounting data on the private firm, and the comparable information on earnings changes for the average S&P 500 company during the same period.

Year	Net Income of Private Company	Earnings Change-Average Firm in the S&P 500
1988	$10.00 million	+ 7%
1989	$15.00 million	+10%
1990	$18.00 million	+ 5%
1991	$18.50 million	- 10%
1992	$19.00 million	- 8%
1993	$22.00 million	+ 6%

A. Estimate the accounting beta for the private company.

B. What are the limitations of an "accounting" beta?

Question 9 - CAPM: Betas and Mergers

The following are the betas of three companies involved in a merger battle. The target firm is Paramount Communications, and the competing bidders are QVC and Viacom:

Company	Beta	Market Value of Equity	Debt
Paramount	1.05	$6,500 million	$817 million
QVC	1.70	$2,000 million	$100 million
Viacom	1.15	$7,500 million	$2,500 million

(Assume that all firms have a tax rate of 35%.)

A. If QVC acquires Paramount, using a mix of debt and equity comparable to its current debt/equity ratio, what would the beta of the combined firm be?

B. If QVC acquires Paramount, using only debt, what would the beta of the comparable firm be?

C. If Viacom acquires Paramount, using a mix of debt and equity comparable to its current debt/equity ratio, what would the beta of the combined firm be?

D. If Viacom acquires Paramount, using only equity, what would the beta of the comparable firm be?

Question 10 - Arbitrage Pricing Model

Consider the following derivation of the arbitrage pricing model, where the expected return on a stock is written as the function of four variables:

$$E(R_j) = 0.062 - 1.855\ \beta_1 + 1.4450\ \beta_2 - 0.124\ \beta_3 - 2.744\ \beta_4$$

Assume that you have estimated the betas relative to each of the four factors for Paramount to be:

$$\beta_1 = -0.07 \qquad \beta_2 = 0.01 \qquad \beta_3 = 0.02 \qquad \beta_4 = 0.01$$

A. What does the intercept of this regression measure?

B. What economic and statistical significance do the four factors have?

C. What do the factor coefficients and betas measure?

D. What is the expected return on Paramount, using the arbitrage pricing model?

E. The beta for Paramount is 1.05. Assuming a risk-free rate of 6.25%, what would your estimate of expected return be under the CAPM? Why is it different from your answer in part (D)?

Question 11 - Dividend Growth Model

The following is a list of companies, with prices, dividends per share and expected growth rates in dividends (from analyst projections) for each company:

Company	Market Price	Current DPS	Growth Rate in DPS	Beta
Merck	$32.00	$1.06	15.0%	1.10
Ogden Co.	$25.00	$1.25	4.0%	1.30
Honda (ADR)	$25.00	$0.27	10.0%	0.75
Microsoft	$84.00	$0.00	NMF	1.30

(Microsoft has an expected growth rate in earnings of 24% for the next five years.)

A. Estimate the cost of equity using the dividend growth model. Which, if any, of these firms may be reasonable candidates for using this model? Why?

B. Estimate the cost of equity using the CAPM. (The thirty-year bond rate is 6.25%.)

C. Which estimate will you use in valuation and why?

Question 12 - WACC Calculation

Merck & Company has 1.13 billion shares traded at a market value of $32 per share, and $1.918 billion in book value of outstanding debt (with an estimated market value of $2 billion). The equity has a book value of $5.5 billion, and the stock has a beta of 1.10. The firm paid interest expenses of $160 million in the most recent financial year, is rated AAA and paid 35% of its income as taxes. The thirty-year government bond rate is 6.25%, and AAA bonds trade at a spread of twenty basis points (0.2%) over the treasury bond rate.

A. What are the market value and book value weights on debt and equity?

B. What is the cost of equity?

C. What is the after-tax cost of debt?

D. What is the cost of capital?

Question 13 - WACC: Another exercise

General Motors has 710 million shares trading at $55 per share and $69 billion in debt outstanding (with a market value of $65 billion), on which it incurred an interest expense of $5 billion in the most recent year. It also has $4 billion in preferred stock outstanding, trading at par, on which it paid a dividend of \$365 million. The stock has a beta of 1.10 and is rated A (which commands a spread of 1.25% over the treasury bond rate of 6.25%). The company faced a corporate tax rate of 40%.

  A. What is the cost of equity for GM?

  B. What is the after-tax cost of debt for GM?

  C. What is the cost of preferred stock?

  D. What is the cost of capital?

CHAPTER 4

ESTIMATION OF CASH FLOWS

Much of the tedium in valuation is associated with estimating cash flows, a necessary element of discounted cash flow valuation. This chapter examines the process of estimating cash flows and establishes some general principles which should be adhered to in all valuation models. The one overriding principle governing cash flow estimation is the need to match cash flows to discount rates: equity cash flows to cost of equity; firm cash flows to cost of capital; pre-tax cash flows to pre-tax rates; post-tax cash flows to post-tax rates; nominal cash flows to nominal rates; and real cash flows to real rates. The process of estimating these cash flows is explained in detail in the pages that follow.

Question 1 - Cash Flows to Equity: Concepts
Which of the following is the best description of the free cash flow to equity?
  A. It is the cash that equity investors can take out of the firm.
  B. It is the dividend that is paid to stockholders.
  C. It is the cash that equity investors can take out of the firm after financing investment needed to sustain future growth.
  D. It is the cash left over after meeting debt payments and paying taxes.
  E. None of the above.

Question 2 - Cash Flows: Concepts
Answer true or false to the following statements.
  A. The free cash flow to equity will always be higher than the net income of the firm, because depreciation is added back.
  B. The free cash flow to equity will always be higher than the dividend.

C. The free cash flow to equity will always be higher than cash flow to the firm, because the latter is a pre-debt cash flow.

D. The entire free cash flow to equity cannot be paid out as a dividend because some of it has to be invested in new projects.

Question 3 - The Effects of Inflation

Answer true or false to the following statements relating to the effect of inflation on cash flows and value.

A. Discounting nominal cash flows at the real discount rate will result in too low an estimate of value.

B. Dicounting real cash flows at the nominal discount rate will result in too low an estimate of value.

C. If done right, the value estimated should be the same if either real cash flows are discounted at the real discount rate or nominal cash flows are discounted at the nominal discount rate.

D. If companies can raise prices at the same rate as inflation, their value should not be affected by changes in the inflation rate.

E. Inflation should increase the value of stocks because it increases expected future cash flows.

Question 4 - Estimating Cash Flows: Diebold Incorporated

Diebold Incorporated manufactures, markets, and services automated teller machines in the United States. The following are selected numbers from the financial statements for 1992 and 1993 (in millions):

	1992	1993
Revenues	$544.0	$620.0
(Less) Operating Expenses	($465.1)	($528.5)
(Less) Depreciation	($12.5)	($14.0)
= Earnings before Interest and Taxes	$66.4	$77.5

(Less) Interest Expenses	($0.0)	($0.0)
(Less) Taxes	($25.3)	($29.5)
= Net Income	$41.1	$48.0
Working Capital	$175.0	$240.0

The firm had capital expenditures of $15 million in 1992 and $18 million in 1993. The working capital in 1991 was $180 million.

A. Estimate the cash flows to equity in 1992 and 1993.

B. What would the cash flows to equity in 1993 have been if working capital had remained at the same percentage of revenue it was in 1992.

Question 5 - Estimating Cash Flows: Ryder System

Ryder System is a full-service truck leasing, maintenance, and rental firm with operations in North America and Europe. The following are selected numbers from the financial statements for 1992 and 1993 (in millions).

	1992	1993
Revenues	$5,192.0	$5,400.0
(Less) Operating Expenses	($3,678.5)	($3848.0)
(Less) Depreciation	($573.5)	($580.0)
= EBIT	$940.0	$972.0
(Less) Interest Expenses	($170.0)	($172.0)
(Less) Taxes	($652.1)	($670.0)
= Net Income	$117.9	$130.0
Working Capital	$92.0	<$370.0>
Total Debt	$2,000 mil	$2,200 mil

The firm had capital expenditures of $800 million in 1992 and $850 million in 1993. The working capital in 1991 was $34.8 million, and the total debt outstanding in 1991 was $1.75 billion. There were 77 million shares outstanding, trading at $29 per share.

A. Estimate the cash flows to equity in 1992 and 1993.

B. Estimate the cash flows to the firm in 1992 and 1993.

C. Assuming that revenues and all expenses (including depreciation and capital expenditures) increase 6%, and that working capital remains unchanged in 1994, estimate the projected cash flows to equity and the firm in 1994. (The firm is assumed to be at its optimal financial leverage.)

D. How would your answer in (c) change if the firm planned to increase its debt ratio in 1994 by financing 75% of its capital expenditures (net of depreciation) with new debt issues?

Question 6 - Estimating Cash Flows: Occidental Petroleum

Occidental Petroleum produces and markets crude oil. The following are selected numbers from the financial statements for 1992 and 1993 (in millions).

	1992	1993
Revenues	$8,494.0	$9,000.0
(Less) Operating Expenses	($6,424.0)	($6,970.0)
(Less) Depreciation	($872.0)	($860.0)
= EBIT	$1,198.0	$1,170.0
(Less) Interest Expenses	($510.0)	($515.0)
(Less) Taxes	($362.0)	($420.0)
= Net Income	$326.0	$235.0
Working Capital	($45.0)	($50.0)

Total Debt $5.4 billion $5.0 billion

The firm had capital expenditures of $950 million in 1992 and $1 billion in 1993. The working capital in 1991 was $190 million, and the total debt outstanding in 1991 was $5.75 billion. There were 305 million shares outstanding, trading at $21 per share.

A. Estimate the cash flows to equity in 1992 and 1993.

B. Estimate the cash flows to the firm in 1992 and 1993.

C. Assuming that revenues and all expenses (including depreciation and capital expenditures) increase 4%, and that working capital remains unchanged in 1994, estimate the projected cash flows to equity and the firm in 1994. (The firm is assumed to be at its optimal financial leverage.)

D. How would your answer in (c) change if the firm planned to reduce its debt ratio in 1994 by financing 100% of its capital expenditures (net of depreciation) with new equity issues?

Question 7 - Inflation and Value

Watts Industries, a manufacturer of valves for industrial and residential use, had the following projected free cash flows to equity per share for the next five years , in nominal terms.

Year	FCFE/share	Terminal Value
1	$1.12	
2	$1.25	
3	$1.40	
4	$1.57	
5	$1.76	$23.32

The terminal price is based upon a stable nominal growth rate of 6% a year after year 5. The discount rate, based upon financial market rates, is 14%, and the expected inflation rate is 3%.

A. Estimate the value per share, using nominal cash flows and the nominal discount rate.

B. Estimate the value per share, using real cash flows and the real discount rate.

Question 8 - After-tax and Pre-tax Valuation

Consider the example of Polaroid Corporation. The stock is trading at $37.00 per share currently. The expected dividends, prior to personal taxes, as well as the expected terminal price, are given below:

Year	Expected DPS	Terminal Price
1	$0.67	
2	$0.75	
3	$0.84	
4	$0.94	
5	$1.06	$62.79

The expected return, prior to personal taxes, on Polaroid is 13%, of which 1.81% is expected to come from dividends. An investor facing a tax rate of 36% on dividends and 25% on capital gains is considering investing in the stock.

A. What is the expected return, after personal taxes, to this investor?

B. What are the expected dividends and terminal price, after personal taxes, to this investor?

C. What is the value of the stock, using these after-personal-tax cash flows and discount rates?

D. What is the value of the stock, using the pre-personal-tax cash flows and discount rates?

Question 9 - Terminal Values for Cash Flow Calculation

The terminal value in a capital budgeting project is generally much lower than the initial investment. The terminal price in a stock valuation is generally much higher than the initial investment. How would you explain the difference?

CHAPTER 5

ESTIMATION OF GROWTH RATES

The value of a firm is ultimately determined not by current cash flows but by expected future cash flows. The estimation of growth rates in earnings and cash flows is therefore central to doing a reasonable valuation. Growth rates can be obtained in many ways: they can be based upon past growth; drawn from estimates made by other analysts who follow the firm; or related to the firm's fundamentals. Since each of these approaches yields some valuable information, it makes sense to blend them to arrive at one composite growth rate to use in the valuation. This chapter examines different approaches to estimating future growth, and discusses the determinants of growth.

Question 1 - Arithmetic and Geometric Means

The following are the earnings per share of Thermo Electron, a company that designs cogeneration and resource recovery plants, from 1987 to 1992:

Year	EPS
1987	0.67
1988	0.77
1989	0.90
1990	1.10
1991	1.31
1992	1.51

A. Estimate the arithmetic average growth rate in earnings per share from 1987 to 1992.

B. Estimate the geometric average growth rate in earnings per share from 1987 to 1992.

C. Why are the growth rates different?

Question 2 - Linear and Log-linear Models of Earnings Growth

Consider again the example of Thermo Electron, described in the prior example, using the historical data from 1987 to 1992.

A. Estimate the growth rate from a linear regression model.

B. Estimate the growth rate from a log-linear regression model.

C. Project the earnings per share in 1993 using both models.

Question 3 - Dealing with Negative Earnings

The earnings per share from 1987 to 1993 are reported below for McDonnell Douglas, an aircraft manufacturer with extensive defense contracts:

Year	EPS
1987	7.27
1988	7.91
1989	-0.97
1990	-2.64
1991	8.42
1992	-0.06
1993	10.75

A. Estimate the geometric average growth rate in earnings from 1987 to 1993.

B. Estimate the arithmetic average growth rate in earnings from 1987 to 1993, using a correction for the negative earnings.

C. Estimate the growth rate in earnings, using the linear regression model.

Question 4 - Earnings Growth and ROE

Johnson and Johnson, a leading manufacturer of healthcare products, had a return on equity in 1992 of 31.4%, and paid out 36% of its earnings as dividends. It earned a net income of $1,625 million on a book value of equity of $5,171 million. As a consequence of healthcare reform, it is expected that the return on equity will drop to 25% in 1993 and that the dividend payout ratio will remain unchanged.

A. Estimate the growth rate in earnings based upon 1992 numbers.

B. Estimate the growth rate in 1993, when the ROE droP/S from 31.4% to 25%.

C. Estimate the growth rate after 1993, assuming that 1993 numbers can be sustained.

Question 5 - Earnings Growth, Leverage, and Risk

Eastman Kodak was, in the view of many observers, in serious need of restructuring in 1994. In 1993, the firm reported the following:

Net Income	$1,080 million
Interest Expense	$ 550 million

The firm also had the following estimates of debt and equity in the balance sheet:

Equity (Book Value)	$6,000 million
Debt (Book Value)	$6,880 million

The firm also paid out total dividends of $660 million in 1993. The stock was trading at $63, and there were 330 million shares outstanding. (It faced a corporate tax rate of 40%.) Eastman Kodak had a beta of 1.10.

Analysts believe that Kodak could take the following restructuring actions to improve its financial strength:

- It could sell its chemical division, which has a total book value of assets of $2,500 million and has only $100 million in earnings before interest and taxes.
- It could use the cash to pay down debt and improve its bond rating (leading to a decline in the interest rate to 7%).
- It could reduce the dividend payout ratio to 50% and reinvest more back into the business.

A. What is the expected growth rate in earnings, assuming that 1993 numbers remain unchanged?

B. What is the expected growth rate in earnings, if the restructuring plan described above is put into effect?

C. What will the beta of the stock be, if the restructuring plan is put into effect?

Question 6 - Corporate Strategy and Expected Growth

Philip Morris, a leading consumer products company, was forced to cut prices on its Marlboro brand of cigarettes in early 1993 to combat loss of sales to generic competitors. You are attempting to assess the effects on expected growth as a consequence.

In 1992, Philip Morris had earnings before interest and taxes of $10 billion on sales of $60 billion. The firm also had total assets of $30 billion in that year. As a consequence of its price cuts in 1993, the pre-interest profit margin is expected to decline to 9%. The debt/equity ratio is expected to remain unchanged at 1.00, and the interest rate will remain at 6.5%. (The tax rate is 36%.) Philip Morris pays out 65% of its earnings as dividends.

A. Based upon 1992 numbers, what is the expected growth rate in earnings?

B. Assuming that the asset turnover ratio remains unchanged, what will the growth rate in earnings be after the price cuts in 1993?

C. How much will the asset turnover ratio have to increase for Philip Morris to return to the growth rate it had in 1992?

Question 7 - Adjusting Inputs For Firm Type

Computer Associates makes software that enables computers to run more efficiently. It is still in its high-growth phase and has the following financial characteristics:

Return on Assets = 25%

Dividend Payout Ratio = 7%

Debt/Equity Ratio = 10%

Interest rate on Debt = 8.5%

Corporate tax rate = 40%

It is expected to become a stable firm in ten years.

A. What is the expected growth rate for the high-growth phase?

B. Would you expect the financial characteristics of the firm to change once it reaches a steady state? What form do you expect the change to take?

C. Assume now that the industry averages for larger, more stable firms in the industry are as follows:

Industry Average Return on Assets = 14%

Industry Average Debt/Equity Ratio = 40%

Industry Average Interest Rate on Debt = 7%

Industry Average Dividend Payout ratio = 50%

D. What would you expect the growth rate in the stable growth phase to be?

Question 8 - Weighting Different Estimates of Growth Rate

The following are a number of valuation scenarios, where multiple estimates of growth are available. Specify how you weight the different growth rates and why.

A. A cyclical firm, whose earnings have dropped significantly (historical growth rate is negative) as a consequence of a recession, but which you believe has bottomed out and is in the process of recovering. The firm is heavily followed by analysts, who have a good track record in forecasting earnings growth.

B. A troubled firm, whose earnings have dropped significantly because of a combination of bad luck and bad management, but which is now restructuring. You have fairly good information on the form the restructuring will take and its expected impact. Analysts follow the firm, but their track record is spotty.

C. A healthy firm, where the estimates of growth from history, analysts, and fundamentals are fairly close.

D. A firm, which has a long and fairly reliable history of earnings growth, but which has just sold off three divisions (comprising almost half of the market value of the firm). Analysts follow the stock, but base forecasts primarily on historical growth.

CHAPTER 6

DIVIDEND DISCOUNT MODELS

The basic model for valuing equity is the dividend discount model: the value of a stock is the present value of its expected dividends. This chapter explores the general model and its permutations tailored for different assumptions about future growth. It also examines issues in using the dividend discount model and the results of studies that have looked at its efficacy.

Question 1 - Uses of the Dividend Discount Model

Respond true or false to the following statements relating to the dividend discount model.

A. The dividend discount model cannot be used to value a high growth company that pays no dividends.

B. The dividend discount model will undervalue stocks, because it is too conservative.

C. The dividend discount model will find more undervalued stocks, when the overall stock market is depressed.

D. Stocks that are undervalued using the dividend discount model have generally made significant positive excess returns over long periods (five years or more).

E. Stocks which pay high dividends and have low price/earnings ratios are more likely to come out as undervalued using the dividend discount model.

Question 2 - Gordon Growth Model : Concepts

An analyst complains that the Gordon Growth Model yields absurd results. He presents several problems that he has had with the model. Respond to each of these comments.

A. The model values stocks which do not pay dividends at zero.

B. The model sometimes yields negative values for stocks, when growth rates exceed the discount rate.

C. The model yields absurdly high values for other stocks, where the discount rate is very close to the growth rate.

D. No firm raises dividends by a fixed percent every year. The model's assumption is unrealistic and the values obtained from it will not hold.

E. Since cyclical firms have earnings which go up and down, based upon economic conditions, the model can never be used to value a cyclical firm.

Question 3 - Gordon Growth Model

Ameritech Corporation paid dividends per share of $3.56 in 1992, and dividends are expected to grow 5.5% a year forever. The stock has a beta of 0.90, and the treasury bond rate is 6.25%.

A. What is the value per share, using the Gordon Growth Model?

B. The stock is trading for $80 per share. What would the growth rate in dividends have to be to justify this price?

Question 4 - Growth Rate in the Gordon Growth Model

A key input for the Gordon Growth Model is the expected growth rate in dividends over the long term. How, if at all, would you factor in the following considerations in estimating this growth rate?

A. There is an increase in the inflation rate.

B. The economy in which the firm operates is growing very rapidly.

C. The growth potential of the industry in which the firm operates is very high.

D. The current management of the firm is of very high quality.

Question 5 - Two-Stage Dividend Discount Model: Basics

Newell Corporation, a manufacturer of do-it-yourself hardware and housewares, reported earnings per share of $2.10 in 1993, on which it paid dividends per share of $0.69. Earnings are expected to grow 15% a year from 1994 to 1998, during which period the dividend payout ratio is expected to remain unchanged. After 1998, the earnings growth rate is expected to drop to a stable 6%, and the payout ratio is expected to increase to 65% of earnings. The firm has a beta of 1.40 currently, and it is expected to have a beta of 1.10 after 1998. The treasury bond rate is 6.25%.

A. What is the expected price of the stock at the end of 1998?

B. What is the value of the stock, using the two-stage dividend discount model?

Question 6 - Two-Stage Dividend Discount Model: Estimating Terminal Payout Ratio

Church & Dwight, a large producer of sodium bicarbonate, reported earnings per share of $1.50 in 1993 and paid dividends per share of $0.42. In 1993, the firm also reported the following:

Net Income   = $30 million

Interest Expense = $0.8 million

Book Value of Debt = $7.6 million

Book Value of Equity = $160 million

The firm faced a corporate tax rate of 38.5%. (The market value debt-to-equity ratio is 5%.) The treasury bond rate is 7%.

The firm expects to maintain these financial fundamentals from 1994 to 1998, after which its is expected to become a stable firm, with an earnings growth rate of 6%. The firm's financial characteristics will approach industry averages after 1998. The industry averages are as follows:

Return on Assets = 12.5%

Debt/Equity Ratio = 25%

Interest Rate on Debt = 7%

Church and Dwight had a beta of 0.85 in 1993, and the unlevered beta is not expected to change over time.

A. What is the expected growth rate in earnings, based upon fundamentals, for the high-growth period (1994 to 1998)?

B. What is the expected payout ratio after 1998?

C. What is the expected beta after 1998?

D. What is the expected price at the end of 1998?

E. What is the value of the stock, using the two-stage dividend discount model?

F. How much of this value can be attributed to extraordinary growth? to stable growth?

Question 7 - The H Model

Oneida Inc. the world's largest producer of stainless steel and silver plated flatware, reported earnings per share of $0.80 in 1993, and paid dividends per share of $0.48 in that year. The firm is expected to report earnings growth of 25% in 1994, after which the growth rate is expected to decline linearly over the following six years to 7% in 1999. The stock is expected to have a beta of 0.85. (The treasury bond rate is 6.25%.)

A. Estimate the value of stable growth, using the H Model.

B. Estimate the value of extraordinary growth, using the H Model.

C. What are the assumptions about dividend payout in the H Model?

Question 8 - The Three-Stage Dividend Discount Model

Medtronic Inc., the world's largest manufacturer of implantable biomedical devices, reported earnings per share in 1993 of $3.95, and paid dividends per share of $0.68. Its earnings are expected to grow 16% from 1994 to 1998, but the growth rate is expected to decline each year after that to a stable growth rate of 6% in 2003. The payout ratio is expected to remain unchanged from 1994 to 1998, after which it will increase each year to reach 60% in steady state. The stock is expected to have a beta of 1.25 from 1994 to 1998, after which the beta will decline each year to reach 1.00 by the time the firm becomes stable. (The treasury bond rate is 6.25%.)

A. Assuming that the growth rate declines linearly (and the payout ratio increases linearly) from 1999 to 2003, estimate the dividends per share each year from 1994 to 2003.

B. Estimate the expected price at the end of 2003.

C. Estimate the value per share, using the three-stage dividend discount model.

CHAPTER 7

FREE CASH FLOW TO EQUITY DISCOUNT MODELS

The dividend discount model is based upon the premise that the only cash flows received by stockholders are dividends. This chapter uses a more expansive definition of cash flows to equity as the cash flows left over after meeting all financial obligations, including debt payments, and after covering capital expenditure and working capital needs. It discusses the reasons for differences between dividends and free cash flows to equity, and presents the discounted free cash flow to equity model for valuation.

Question 1 - FCFE Calculation: Concepts
Respond true or false to the following statements relating to the calculation and use of FCFE.

A. The free cash flow to equity will generally be more volatile than dividends.

B. The free cash flow to equity will always be higher than the dividends.

C. The free cash flow to equity will always be higher than net income.

D. The free cash flow to equity can never be negative.

Question 2 - Constant Growth FCFE Model
Kimberly-Clark, a household product manufacturer, reported earnings per share of $3.20 in 1993, and paid dividends per share of $1.70 in that year. The firm reported depreciation of $315 million in 1993, and capital expenditures of $475 million. (There were 160 million shares outstanding, trading at $51 per share.) This ratio of capital expenditures to depreciation is expected to be maintained in the long term. The working

capital needs are negligible. Kimberly-Clark had debt outstanding of $1.6 billion, and intends to maintain its current financing mix (of debt and equity) to finance future investment needs. The firm is in steady state and earnings are expected to grow 7% a year. The stock had a beta of 1.05. (The treasury bond rate is 6.25%.)

  A. Estimate the value per share, using the Dividend Discount Model.

  B. Estimate the value per share, using the FCFE Model.

  C. How would you explain the difference between the two models, and which one would you use as your benchmark for comparison to the market price?

Question 3 - Two-Stage FCFE Model: Basics

Ecolab Inc. sells chemicals and systems for cleaning, sanitizing, and maintenance. It reported earnings per share of $2.35 in 1993, and expected earnings growth of 15.5% a year from 1994 to 1998, and 6% a year after that. The capital expenditure per share was $2.25, and depreciation was $1.125 per share in 1993. Both are expected to grow at the same rate as earnings from 1994 to 1998. Working capital is expected to remain at 5% of revenues, and revenues which were $1,000 million in 1993 are expected to increase 6% a year from 1994 to 1998, and 4% a year after that. The firm currently has a debt ratio (D/(D+E)) of 5%, but plans to finance future investment needs (including working capital investments) using a debt ratio of 20%. The stock is expected to have a beta of 1.00 for the period of the analysis, and the treasury bond rate is 6.50%. (There are 63 million shares outstanding.)

  A. Assuming that capital expenditures and depreciation offset each other after 1998, estimate the value per share.

B. Assuming that capital expenditures continue to be 200% of depreciation even after 1998, estimate the value per share.

C. What would the value per share have been, if the firm had continued to finance new investments with its old financing mix (5%)? Is it fair to use the same beta for this analysis?

Question 4 - Two-Stage FCFE Model: An Extended Application

Dionex Corporation, a leader in the development and manufacture of ion chromography systems (used to identify contaminants in electronic devices), reported earnings per share of $2.02 in 1993, and paid no dividends. These earnings are expected to grow 14% a year for five years (1994 to 1998) and 7% a year after that. The firm reported depreciation of $2 million in 1993 and capital spending of $4.20 million, and had 7 million shares outstanding. The working capital is expected to remain at 50% of revenues, which were $106 million in 1993, and are expected to grow 6% a year from 1994 to 1998 and 4% a year after that. The firm is expected to finance 10% of its capital expenditures and working capital needs with debt. Dionex had a beta of 1.20 in 1993, and this beta is expected to drop to 1.10 after 1998. (The treasury bond rate is 7%.)

A. Estimate the expected free cash flow to equity from 1994 to 1998, assuming that capital expenditures and depreciation grow at the same rate as earnings.

B. Estimate the terminal price per share (at the end of 1998). Stable firms in this industry have capital expenditures which are 150% of revenues, and maintain working capital at 25% of revenues.

C. Estimate the value per share today, based upon the FCFE model.

Question 5 - Three-Stage FCFE Model: Manufacturing Firm

Biomet Inc., designs, manufactures and markets reconstructive and trauma devices, and reported earnings per share of $0.56 in 1993, on which it paid no dividends. (It had revenues per share in 1993 of $2.91). It had capital expenditures of $0.13 per share in 1993 and depreciation in the same year of $0.08 per share. The working capital was 60% of revenues in 1993 and will remain at that level from 1994 to 1998, while earnings and revenues are expected to grow 17% a year. The earnings growth rate is expected to decline linearly over the following five years to a rate of 5% in 2003. During the high growth and transition periods, capital spending and depreciation are expected to grow at the same rate as earnings, but are expected to offset each other when the firm reaches steady state. Working capital is expected to drop from 60% of revenues during the 1994-1998 period to 30% of revenues after 2003. The firm has no debt currently, but plans to finance 10% of its net capital investment and working capital requirements with debt.

The stock is expected to have a beta of 1.45 for the high growth period (1994-1998), and it is expected to decline to 1.10 by the time the firm goes into steady state (in 2003). The treasury bond rate is 7%.

A. Estimate the value per share, using the FCFE model.

B. Estimate the value per share, assuming that working capital stays at 60% of revenues forever.

C. Estimate the value per share, assuming that the beta remains unchanged at 1.45 forever.

Question 6 - Three-Stage FCFE Model: Service Firm

Omnicare Inc., which provides pharmacy management and drug therapy to nursing homes, reported earnings per share of $0.85 in 1993 on revenues per share of $12.50. It had negligible capital expenditures, which were covered by depreciation, but had to maintain working capital at 40% of revenues. Revenues and earnings are expected to grow 20% a year from 1994 to 1998, after which the growth rate is expected to decline linearly over three years to 5% in 2001. The firm has a debt ratio of 15%, which it intends to maintain in the future. The stock has a beta of 1.10, which is expected to remain unchanged for the period of the analysis. The treasury bond rate is 7%.

A. Estimate the value per share, using the free cash flow to equity model.

B. Assume now that you find out that the way that Omnicare is going to create growth is by giving easier credit terms to their clients. How would that affect your estimate of value? (Will it increase or decrease?)

C. How sensitive is your estimate of value to changes in the working capital assumption?

Question 7- FCFE Model and Dividend Discount Model

Which of the following firms is likely to have a higher value from the dividend discount model, a higher value from the FCFE model or the same value from both models?

A. A firm that pays out less in dividends than it has available in FCFE, but which invests the balance in treasury bonds.

B. A firm which pays out more in dividends than it has available in FCFE, and then issues stock to cover the difference.

C. A firm which pays out, on average, its FCFE as dividends.

D. A firm which pays out less in dividends that it has available in FCFE, but which uses the cash at regular intervals to acquire other firms, with the intent of diversifying.

E. A firm which pays out more in dividends than it has available in FCFE, but borrows money to cover the difference. (The firm is already over-levered.)

CHAPTER 8

VALUING A FIRM - THE FREE CASH FLOW TO FIRM (FCFF) APPROACH

There are two approaches to valuing the equity in the firm: the dividend discount model and the FCFE valuation model. This chapter develops another approach to valuation where the entire firm is valued, by discounting the cumulated cash flows to all claim holders in the firm by the weighted average cost of capital, and examines its limitations and applications.

Question 1 - Free Cash Flow to the Firm: Concepts
Respond true or false to the following statements about the free cash flow to the firm.

A. The free cash flow to the firm is always higher than the free cash flow to equity.

B. The free cash flow to the firm is the cumulated cash flow to all investors in the firm, though the form of their claims may be different.

C. The free cash flow to the firm is a pre-debt, pre-tax cash flow.

D. The free cash flow to the firm is an after-debt, after-tax cash flow.

E. The free cash flow to the firm cannot be estimated without knowing interest and principal payments, for a firm with debt.

Question 2 - Free Cash Flow to Firm and Other Definitions of FCFF
Lay out how you would get to the free cash flow to the firm (what would you add and/or subtract to the base number?) from the following measures of cash flow.

A. Net Income

B. Earnings before taxes

C. EBIT (Earnings before interest and taxes)

D. EBITDA (Earnings before interest, taxes, and depreciation)

E. Net Operating Income

F. Free Cash Flow to Equity

Question 3 - FCFF Steady State Model

Union Pacific Railroad reported net income of $770 million in 1993, after interest expenses of $320 million. (The corporate tax rate was 36%.) It reported depreciation of $960 million in that year, and capital spending was $1.2 billion. The firm also had $4 billion in debt outstanding on the books, rated AA (carrying a yield to maturity of 8%), trading at par (up from $3.8 billion at the end of 1992). The beta of the stock is 1.05, and there were 200 million shares outstanding (trading at $60 per share), with a book value of $5 billion. Union Pacific paid 40% of its earnings as dividends and working capital requirements are negligible. (The treasury bond rate is 7%.)

A. Estimate the free cash flow to the firm in 1993.

B. Estimate the value of the firm at the end of 1993.

C. Estimate the value of equity at the end of 1993, and the value per share, using the FCFF approach.

Question 4 - Two-Stage FCFF Model: Lockheed Corporation

Lockheed Corporation, one of the largest defense contractors in the U.S., reported EBITDA of $1290 million in 1993, prior to interest expenses of $215 million and depreciation charges of $400 million. Capital Expenditures in 1993 amounted to $450 million, and working capital was 7% of revenues (which were $13,500 million). The firm had debt outstanding of $3.068 billion (in book value terms), trading at a market value of $3.2 billion, and yielding a pre-tax interest rate of 8%. There were 62 million shares outstanding, trading at $64 per share, and the most recent beta is 1.10. The tax rate for the firm is 40%. (The treasury bond rate is 7%.)

The firm expects revenues, earnings, capital expenditures and depreciation to grow at 9.5% a year from 1994 to 1998, after which the growth rate is expected to drop to 4%. (Capital spending will offset depreciation in the steady state period.) The company also plans to lower its debt/equity ratio to 50% for the steady state (which will result in the pre-tax interest rate dropping to 7.5%.)

A. Estimate the value of the firm.

B. Estimate the value of the equity in the firm and the value per share.

Question 5 - Valuing a Division

In the face of disappointing earnings results and increasingly assertive institutional stockholders, Eastman Kodak was considering a major restructuring in 1993. As part of this restructuring, it was considering the sale of its health division, which earned $560 million in earnings before interest and taxes in 1993, on revenues of $5.285 billion. The expected growth in earnings was expected to moderate to 6% between 1994 and 1998, and to 4% after that. Capital expenditures in the health division amounted to $420 million in 1993, while depreciation was $350 million. Both are expected to grow 4% a year in the long term. Working capital requirements are negligible.

The average beta of firms competing with Eastman Kodak's health division is 1.15. While Eastman Kodak has a debt ratio (D/(D+E)) of 50%, the health division can sustain a debt ratio (D/(D+E)) of only 20%, which is similar to the average debt ratio of firms competing in the health sector. At this level of debt, the health division can expect to pay

7.5% on its debt, before taxes. (The tax rate is 40%, and the treasury bond rate is 7%.)

A. Estimate the cost of capital for the division.

B. Estimate the value of the division.

C. Why might an acquirer pay more than this estimated value?

Question 6- Choosing the Optimal Leverage

Santa Fe Pacific, a major rail operator with diversified operations, had earnings before interest, taxes and depreciation, of $637 million in 1993, with depreciation amounting to $235 million (offset by capital expenditure of an equivalent amount). The firm is in steady state and expected to grow 6% a year in perpetuity. Santa Fe Pacific had a beta of 1.25 in 1993 and debt outstanding of $1.34 billion. The stock price was $18.25 at the end of 1993, and there were 183.1 million shares outstanding. The expected ratings and the costs of debt at different levels of debt for Santa Fe are shown in the following table (the treasury bond rate is 7%, and the firm faced a tax rate of 40%):

D/(D+E)	Rating	Cost of Debt (Pre-tax)
0%	AAA	6.23%
10%	AAA	6.23%
20%	A+	6.93%
30%	A-	7.43%
40%	BB	8.43%
50%	B+	8.93%
60%	B-	10.93%
70%	CCC	11.93%
80%	CCC	11.93%
90%	CC	13.43%

The earnings before interest and taxes are expected to grow 3% a year in perpetuity, with capital expenditures offset by depreciation. (The tax rate is 40% and the treasury bond rate is 7%.)

A. Estimate the cost of capital at the current debt ratio.

B. Estimate the costs of capital at debt ratios ranging from 0% to 90%.

C. Estimate the value of the firm at debt ratios ranging from 0% to 90%.

Question 7 - Choosing the Optimal Leverage and Moving There

Bally's Manufacturing, a large leisure-time company, that owns three casinos in Las Vegas and over 300 fitness centers had debt outstanding of $1.180 billion in 1993, and 45.99 million shares outstanding, trading at $9 per share. The debt is rated B-, and commands a pre-tax interest rate of 10.31%. The company had $236 million in earnings before interest, taxes and depreciation in 1993, and depreciation of $109 million. (Capital expenditures amounted to $125 million in 1993.) The stock had a beta of 2.20.

Bally's is planning to pay down debt and reduce its debt ratio (D/(D+E)) to 50%, which should raise its debt rating to A (and lower the pre-tax rate to 7.51%). The tax rate for the firm is 40%. The treasury bond rate is 7%.

A. What is Ballys' current cost of capital?

B. What will the effect of the debt reduction be on the cost of capital?

C. The firm value is expected to increase by $100 million as a consequence of the debt reduction. Assuming that the firm is in steady state, what is the expected growth rate in cash flows to the firm that will yield this value increase?

CHAPTER 9

SPECIAL CASES IN VALUATION

The standard discounted cash flow valuation models have to be modified in special cases - for cyclical firms, for troubled firms, for firms with special product options and for private firms. This chapter examines the problems associated with valuing these firms and suggests possible solutions.

Question 1 - Cyclical Firm: Normalized Earnings Per Share

Intermet Corporation, the largest independent iron foundry organization in the country, reported a deficit per share of $0.15 in 1993. The earnings per share from 1984 to 1992, were as follows:

Year	EPS
1984	$0.69
1985	$0.71
1986	$0.90
1987	$1.00
1988	$0.76
1989	$0.68
1990	$0.09
1991	$0.16
1992	<$0.07>

The firm had capital expenditures of $1.60 per share, and depreciation per share of $1.20 in 1993. Working capital was expected to increase $0.10 per share in 1994. The stock has a beta of 1.2, which is expected to remain unchanged, and finances its capital expenditure and working capital requirements with 40% debt. (D/(D+E)). The firm is expected, in the long term, to grow at the same rate as the economy (6%).

A. Estimate the normalized earnings per share in 1994, using the average earnings approach.

B. Estimate the normalized free cash flow to equity per share in 1994, using the average earnings approach.

C. The firm is expected, in the long term, to grow at the same rate as the economy (6%).

Question 2 - Valuing a Cyclical Firm: Normalized Earnings (ROA)

General Motors Corporation reported a deficit per share in 1993 of $4.85, following losses in the two earlier years (the average earnings per share is negative). The company had assets with a book value of $25 billion, and spent almost $7 billion on capital expenditures in 1993, which was partially offset by a depreciation charge of $6 billion. The firm had $19 billion in debt outstanding, on which it paid interest expenses of $1.4 billion. It intends to maintain a debt ratio (D/(D+E)) of 50%. The working capital requirements of the firm are negligible, and the stock has a beta of 1.10. In the last normal period of operations for the firm between 1986 and 1989, the firm earned an average return on assets of 12%. (The tax rate was 40%.) The treasury bond rate is 7%.

Once earnings are normalized, GM expects them to grow 5% a year forever, and capital expenditures and depreciation to keep track.

A. Estimate the value per share for GM, assuming earnings are normalized instantaneously.

B. How would your valuation be affected if GM is not going to reach its normalized earnings until 1995 (in two years)?

Question 3 - Valuing a Cyclical Firm: Adjusted Growth Rate

Chrysler Corporation reported a significant loss of $2.74 per share in 1991, but reported positive earnings per share of $1.38 in 1992, as sales improved and profit margins increased. The improving economy is expected to quadruple earnings in 1993, after which earnings growth is expected to stabilize at 5% in the long term. Chrysler also reported capital spending per share of $5.50 and depreciation per share of $4.50 in 1992, and both items are expected to grow 5% a year in the long term. The working capital for the firm amounted to $2.50 per share in 1992, and was expected to grow 3% a year in the long term. The beta for the stock is 1.25, but is expected to stabilize at 1.10 after 1993. The firm expects to maintain a debt ratio of 40%. The treasury bond rate is 7%.

A. Estimate the value per share.

B. How sensitive is this estimate to assumptions about growth in 1993?

Question 4 - Valuing a Troubled Firm: Using Bond Rating

Toro Corporation, which manufactures lawn mowers and tractors, had revenues of $635 million in 1992, on which it reported a loss of $7 million (largely as a consequence of the recession). It had interest expenses of $17 million in 1992, and its bonds were rated BBB. [A typical BBB rated company had an interest coverage ratio (EBIT/Interest Expenses) of 3.10.] The company faced a 40% tax rate. The stock had a beta of 1.10. The treasury bond rate is 7%.

Toro spent $25 million on capital expenditures in 1992, and had depreciation of $20 million. Working capital amounted to 25% of sales. The company expects to maintain a debt ratio of 25%. In the long term, growth in revenues and profits is expected to be 4%, once earnings return to normal levels.

A. Assuming that the bond rating reflects normalized earnings, estimate the normalized earnings for Toro Corporation.

B. Allowing for the long-term growth rate on normalized earnings, estimate the value of equity for Toro Corporation.

Question 5 - Valuing a Troubled Firm: Normalized Earnings

Kollmorgen Corporation, a diversified technology company, reported sales of $194.9 million in 1992, and had a net loss of $1.9 million in that year. Its net income had traced a fairly volatile course over the previous five years:

Year	Net Income
1987	$0.3 million
1988	$11.5 million
1989	-$2.4 million
1990	$7.2 million
1991	-$4.6 million

The stock had a beta of 1.20, and the normalized net income is expected to increase 6% a year until 1996, after which the growth rate is expected to stabilize at 5% a year (the beta will drop to 1.00). The depreciation amounted to $8 million in 1992, and capital spending amounted to $10 million in that year. Both items are expected to grow 5% a year in the long term. The firm expects to maintain a debt ratio of 35%. (The treasury bond rate is 7%.)

A. Assuming that the average earnings from 1987 to 1992 represents the normalized earnings, estimate the normalized earnings and free cash flow to equity.

B. Estimate the value per share.

Question 6 - Valuing a Troubled Firm: Operating Margin

Delta Airlines, the third ranking domestic airline, had revenues of $12 billion in 1993 and reported a loss of $415 million in that year. Between 1988 and 1990, which was the last period of significant profitability for the firm, the firm had a pre-tax operating margin of 12% (Pre-tax Operating Margin = EBIT/Sales). Delta Airlines had interest expenses of $340 million in 1993, and its capital expenditures were offset by depreciation. The company faces a tax rate of 40%. The stock had a beta of 1.15, and the treasury bond rate is 7%. Working capital requirements are negligible.

The expected growth rate in revenues/net incomes is 6% in the long term.

A. Assuming that the firm returns to 1988-90 levels of profitability by 1994, estimate the value of equity.

B. Estimate the value of equity, if the firm does not return to 1988-90 levels of profitability until 1995. (The firm continues to lose money in 1994.)

Question 7 - Valuing a Troubled Firm: FCFF Approach

OHM Corporation, an environmental service provider, had revenues of $209 million in 1992 and reported losses of $3.1 million. It had earnings before interest and taxes of $12.5 million in 1992, and had debt outstanding of $109 million (in market value terms). There are 15.9 million shares outstanding, trading at $11 per share. The pre-tax interest rate on debt owed by the firm is 8.5%, and the stock has a beta of 1.15. The firm's EBIT is expected to increase 10% a year from 1993 to 1996, after which the growth rate is expected to drop to 4% in the long term. Capital expenditures will be offset by depreciation, and working capital needs are negligible. (The corporate tax rate is 40%, and the treasury bond rate is 7%.)

A. Estimate the cost of capital for OHM.

B. Estimate the value of the firm.

C. Estimate the value of equity (both total and on a per share basis).

Question 8 - Valuing a Private Firm

You have been asked by the owner of a small firm that produces and sells computer software to estimate the value of his firm. The firm had revenues of $20 million in the most recent year, on which it made earnings before interest and taxes of $2 million. The firm had debt outstanding of $10 million, on which pre-tax interest expenses amounted to $1 million. The book value of equity is $10 million. The average beta of publicly traded firms that are in the same business is 1.30, and the average debt-equity ratio is 0.2 (based upon the market value of equity). The market value of equity of these firms is, on average, three times the book value of equity. All firms face a 40% tax rate. Capital expenditures amounted to $1 million in the most recent year, and were twice the depreciation charge in that year. Both items are expected to grow at the same rate as revenues for the next five years, and to offset each other in steady state.

The revenues of this firm are expected to grow 20% a year for the next five years, and 5% after that. Net income is expected to increase 25% a year for the next five years, and 8% after that. The treasury bond rate is 7%.

A. Estimate the cost of equity for this private firm.

B. Estimate the cost of capital for this private firm.

C. Estimate the value of the owner's stake in this private firm, using both the firm approach and the equity approach.

Question 9 - Estimating Value: Initial Public Offering

Boston Chicken, a company selling roasted chickens and accompaniments in outlets through the country, went public in 1993. In the year prior to going public, it had revenues of $40 million, on which it reported earnings before interest and taxes of $12 million. The firm had no debt outstanding, and expected revenues to grow 35% a year from 1993 to 1997, 15% a year from 1998 to 2000, and 5% a year after that, while pre-tax operating margins (EBIT/Revenues) were expected to remain stable. Capital expenditures – which exceeded depreciation by $5 million in the year prior to going public – were expected to grow 20% a year from 1993 to 1997, as is depreciation. After 1998, capital expenditures are expected to offset depreciation. Working capital requirements are negligible.

The average beta of publicly traded fast-food chains with which Boston Chicken will be competing is 1.15, and their average debt-equity ratio is 25%. Boston Chicken plans to maintain its policy of no debt until 1997, and to move to the industry average debt ratio after that (the pre-tax cost of debt is expected to be 8%). The treasury bond rate is 7%. All firms face a tax rate of 40%.

A. Estimate the cost of equity for Boston Chicken.

B. Estimate the value of equity for Boston Chicken.

CHAPTER 10

PRICE/EARNINGS MULTIPLES

The price/earnings multiple (P/E) is the most widely used and misused of all multiples. Its simplicity makes it an attractive choice in applications ranging from pricing initial public offerings to making judgments on relative value, but its relationship to a firm's financial fundamentals is often ignored, leading to significant errors in applications. This chapter will try to provide some insight into the determinants of price/earnings ratios.

Question 1 - P/E Ratio for a Stable Firm

National City Corporation, a bank holding company, reported earnings per share of $2.40 in 1993, and paid dividends per share of $1.06. The earnings had grown 7.5% a year over the prior five years, and were expected to grow 6% a year in the long term (starting in 1994). The stock had a beta of 1.05 and traded for ten times earnings. The treasury bond rate was 7%.

A. Estimate the P/E Ratio for National City Corporation.

B. What long term growth rate is implied in the firm's current P/E ratio?

Question 2 - P/E Ratio for a Market

On March 11, 1994, the New York Stock Exchange Composite was trading at 16.9 times earnings, and the average dividend yield across stocks on the exchange was 2.5%. The treasury bond rate on March 11, 1994, was 6.95%. The economy was expected to grow 2.5% a year, in real terms, in the long term, and the consensus estimate for inflation, in the long term, was 3.5%.

A. Based upon these inputs, estimate the appropriate P/E ratio for the exchange.

B. What growth rate in dividends/earnings would justify the P/E ratio on March 11, 1994?

C. Would it matter whether this higher growth comes from higher inflation or higher real growth? Why?

Question 3 - P/E Ratio for a High Growth Firm

International Flavors and Fragrances, a leading creator and manufacturer of flavors and fragrances, paid out dividends of $0.91 per share on earnings per share of $1.64 in 1992. The firm is expected to have a return on equity of 20% between 1993 and 1997, after which the firm is expected to have stable growth of 6% a year (the return on equity is expected to drop to 15% in the stable growth phase.) The dividend payout ratio is expected to remain at the current level from 1993 to 1997. The stock has a beta of 1.10, which is not expected to change. The treasury bond rate is 7%.

A. Estimate the P/E ratio for International Flavors, based upon fundamentals.

B. Estimate how much of this P/E ratio can be ascribed to the extraordinary growth in earnings that the firm expects to have between 1993 and 1997.

Question 4 - P/E Ratio as a Function of Growth

Cracker Barrel, which operates restaurants and gift shops, reported dramatic growth in earnings and revenues between 1983 and 1992. During this period, earnings grew from $0.08 per share in 1983 to $0.78 per share in 1993. The dividends paid in 1993 amounted to only $0.02 per share. The earnings growth rate was expected to ease to 15% a year from 1994 to 1998, and to 6% a year after that. The payout ratio is expected to increase to 10% from 1994 to 1998, and to 50% after that. The beta of the stock is currently 1.55, but it is expected to decline to 1.25 for the 1994-98 time period and to 1.10 after that. The treasury bond rate is 7%.

A. Estimate the P/E ratio for Cracker Barrel.

B. Estimate how much higher the P/E ratio would have been, if it had been able to maintain the growth rate in earnings that it had posted between 1983 and 1993. (Assume that the dividend payout ratios are unaffected.)

C. Now assume that disappointing earnings reports in the near future lower the expected growth rate between 1994 and 1998 to 10%. Estimate the P/E ratio. (Again, assume that the dividend payout ratio is unaffected.)

Question 5 - P/E Ratios Across Countries

The following were P/E ratios for some Asian markets in February 1994, with relevant information on interest rates and economic growth:

Emerging Market	P/E Ratio	Interest Rate	Inflation	Real GDP growth
China	18.0	20.00%	17.6%	12.1%
Hong Kong	18.1	4.28%	6.2%	5.5%
India	26.6	8.27%	8.6%	4.5%
Indonesia	24.1	9.50%	8.4%	6.1%
Malaysia	34.6	6.00%	3.4%	8.1%
Philippines	21.5	15.00%	9.1%	2.1%
Singapore	26.2	3.00%	2.8%	10.7%
South Korea	22.0	12.90%	5.8%	6.5%

Emerging Market	P/E Ratio	Interest Rate	Inflation	Real GDP growth
Taiwan	34.0	6.13%	2.9%	6.1%
Thailand	23.5	8.00%	4.9%	7.5%

A. Assuming the dividend payout ratio in each of these countries is 60%, estimate the P/E ratio in South Korea and Thailand, based upon stable growth. (Use a risk premium of 7.5% over the risk-free rate in each country.)

B. Using a regression, establish the relationship between P/E ratios and fundamentals.

C. Based upon the regression, which markets are under and overvalued.

Question 6 - P/E Ratios Across Time

The S&P 500 was trading at 21.2 times earnings on December 31, 1993. On the same day, the dividend yield on the index was 2.74%, and the treasury bond rate was 6%. The expected growth rate in real GNP was 2.5%.

A. Assuming that the S&P 500 is correctly priced, what is the inflation rate implied in the P/E ratio?

B. By February 1994, treasury bond rates had increased to 7%. Estimate the effect on the P/E ratio, if payout ratios and expected growth remain unchanged.

C. Does an increase in interest rates always imply lower prices (and P/E ratios)?

Question 7 - P/E Ratios in a Peer Group

The following were the P/E ratios of firms in the aerospace/defense industry at the end of December, 1993, with additional data on expected growth and risk:

Company	P/E Ratio	Expected Growth	Beta	Payout
Boeing	17.3	3.5%	1.10	28%
General Dynamics	15.5	11.5%	1.25	40%
General Motors - Hughes	16.5	13.0%	0.85	41%
Grumman	11.4	10.5%	0.80	37%
Lockheed Corporation	10.2	9.5%	0.85	37%
Logicon	12.4	14.0%	0.85	11%
Loral Corporation	13.3	16.5%	0.75	23%
Martin Marietta	11.0	8.0%	0.85	22%
McDonnell Douglas	22.6	13.0%	1.15	37%
Northrop	9.5	9.0%	1.05	47%
Raytheon	12.1	9.5%	0.75	28%
Rockwell	13.9	11.5%	1.00	38%
Thiokol	8.7	5.5%	0.95	15%
United Industrial	10.4	4.5%	0.70	50%

A. Estimate the average and median P/E ratios. What, if anything, would these averages tell you?

B. An analyst concludes that Thiokol is undervalued, because its P/E ratio is lower than the industry average. Under what conditions is this statement true? Would you agree with it here?

C. Using a regression, control for differences across firms on risk, growth, and payout. Specify how you would use this regression to spot under and overvalued stocks. What are the limitations of this approach?

Question 8 - Cross-sectional Regression: P/E Ratios

The following was the result of a regression of P/E ratios on growth rates, betas, and payout ratios, for stocks listed on the Value Line Database, in April 1993:

P/E = 18.69 + 0.0695 GROWTH - 0.5082 BETA - 0.4262 PAYOUT

Thus, a stock, with an earnings growth rate of 20%, a beta of 1.15, and a payout ratio of 40%, would have had an expected P/E ratio of
P/E = 18.69 + 0.0695 * 20 - 0.5082 (1.15) - 0.4262 * 0.40 = 19.33

You are attempting to value a private firm, with the following characteristics:

- The firm had net profits of $10 million. It did not pay dividends, but had depreciation allowances of $5 million, and capital expenditures of $12 million, in the most recent year. Working capital requirements were negligible.
- The earnings had grown 25% over the previous five years, and are expected to grow at the same rate over the next five years.
- The average beta of publicly traded firms, in the same line of business, is 1.15, and the average debt/equity ratio of these firms is 25%. (The tax rate is 40%.) The private firm is an all-equity financed firm, with no debt.

A. Estimate the appropriate P/E ratio for this private firm, using the regression.

B. Explain some of your concerns in using this regression in valuation.

Question 9 - P/E Ratio In Investments

Which of the following would you consider the best indicator of an undervalued firm?

A. A firm with a P/E ratio lower than the market average.

B. A firm with a P/E ratio lower than the average P/E ratio for the firm's peer group.

C. A firm with a lower P/E ratio than its peer group, and a lower expected growth rate.

D. A firm with a lower P/E ratio than its peer group a higher expected growth rate, and higher risk.

E. A firm with a lower P/E ratio than its peer group, a lower expected growth rate, and lower risk.

F. A firm with a lower P/E ratio than its peer group, a higher expected growth rate, and lower risk.

Question 10 - Using Price/FCFE Multiple, Value/FCFF Multiple

Grumman Corporation, a producer of military aircraft, reported net income of $120 million in 1993, after paying interest expenses of $19 million. The depreciation allowance in 1993 was $77 million, while capital expenditures amounted to $80 million in the same year. Working capital increased by $15 million in 1993. (The tax rate is 40%.) Grumman finances 10% of its net capital investment and working capital needs using debt.

The free cash flows to equity are expected to grow 10% a year from 1994 to 1998, and 6% a year after that. The stock had a beta of 0.80, and this is expected to remain unchanged. The treasury bond rate is 7%.

A. Estimate the Price/FCFE ratio for the firm.

B. Grumman has $251 million in debt outstanding at the end of 1993. What is the Value/FCFF ratio? the Value/EBITDA ratio? Why are they different from the Price/FCFE ratio?

CHAPTER 11

PRICE/BOOK VALUE MULTIPLES

The relationship between price and book value has always attracted the attention of investors. Stocks selling for well below the book value of equity have generally been considered good candidates for undervalued portfolios, while those selling for more than book value have been targets for overvalued portfolios. This chapter examines the price/book value ratio in more detail, considers the determinants of this ratio, and demonstrates how best to evaluate or estimate the ratio.

Question 1 - Basic Concepts on Price/Book Value Ratios
Answer true or false to the following statements, with a short explanation.

A. A stock that sells for less than book value is undervalued.

B. If a company's return on equity drops, its price/book value ratio will generally drop more than proportionately, i.e., if the return on equity drops by half, the price/book value ratio will drop by more than half.

C. A combination of a low price/book value ratio and a high expected return on equity suggests that a stock is undervalued.

D. Other things remaining equal, a higher growth stock will have a higher price/book value ratio than a lower growth stock.

E. In the Gordon Growth model, firms with higher dividend payout ratios will have higher price/book value ratios.

Question 2 - P/BV Ratio for a Stable Firm
NCH Corporation, which markets cleaning chemicals, insecticides and other products, paid dividends of $2.00 per share in 1993 on earnings of $4.00 per share. The book value of equity per share was $40.00, and

earnings are expected to grow 6% a year in the long term. The stock has a beta of 0.85, and sells for $60 per share. (The treasury bond rate is 7%.)

A. Based upon these inputs, estimate the price/book value ratio for NCH.

B. How much would the return on equity have to increase to justify the price/book value ratio at which NCH sells for currently?

Question 3 - P/BV Ratio for an Industry

You are analyzing the price/book value ratios for firms in the trucking industry, relative to returns on equity and required rates of return. The treasury bond rate is 7%. The data on the companies is provided below:

Company	P/BV	ROE	Beta
Builders Transport	2.00	11.5%	1.00
Carolina Freight	0.60	5.5%	1.20
Consolidated Freight	2.60	12.0%	1.15
J.B. Hunt	2.50	14.5%	1.00
M.S. Carriers	2.50	12.5%	1.15
Roadway Services	3.00	14.0%	1.15
Ryder System	2.25	13.0%	1.05
Xtra Corporation	2.80	16.5%	1.10

A. Compute the average P/BV ratio, return on equity, and beta for the industry.

B. Based upon these averages, are stocks in the industry under or overvalued relative to book values?

Question 4 - P/BV Ratio for a High Growth Firm

United Healthcare, a health maintenance organization, is expected to have earnings growth of 30% for the next five years and 6% after that. The dividend payout ratio will be only 10% during the high growth phase, but will increase to 60% in steady state. The return on equity was 21% in the most recent time period. The stock has a beta of 1.65 currently, but the beta is expected to drop to 1.10 in steady state. (The treasury bond rate is 7.25%.)

A. Estimate the price/book value ratio for United Healthcare, given the inputs above.

B. How sensitive is the price/book value ratio to estimates of growth during the high growth period?

C. United Healthcare trades at a price/book value ratio of 7.00. How long would extraordinary growth have to last (at a 30% annual rate) to justify this P/BV ratio?

Question 5 - Effects of Changing ROE on P/BV Ratios

Johnson and Johnson, a leading manufacturer of health care products, had a return on equity of 31.5% in 1993, and paid out 37% of its earnings as dividends. The stock had a beta of 1.25. (The treasury bond rate is 6%.) The extraordinary growth is expected to last for ten years, after which the growth rate is expected to drop to 6% and the return on equity to 15% (the beta will move to 1).

A. Assuming the return on equity and dividend payout ratio continue at current levels for the high growth period, estimate the P/BV ratio for Johnson and Johnson.

B. As the industry changes, it is believed that Johnson and Johnson's return on equity will drop to 20% for the high growth phase. If they choose to maintain their existing dividend payout ratio, estimate the new P/BV ratio for Johnson and Johnson. (You can assume that the inputs for the steady state period are unaffected.)

Question 6 - P/BV Ratios and ROE

Acuson Inc., a designer and manufacturer of medical diagnostic ultrasound imaging systems, has recorded declining returns on equity from 1988 to 1993:

Year	ROE
1988	27.0%
1989	26.3%
1990	23.9%
1991	21.5%
1992	18.3%
1993	6.3%

The firm had a beta of 1.20 through the entire time period. (For purposes of simplicity, you can assume that the treasury bond rate was 7% each year of the analysis.) The firm pays no dividends currently, but expects to pay 50% of its earnings when it reaches steady state (which is expected to be in 1998), after which the return on equity is expected to be 12%.

A. Estimate the P/BV ratio for each year from 1988 to 1993 (keeping the steady state assumptions unchanged).

B. Would you expect the actual P/BV ratio to drop as quickly? Why or why not?

Question 7 - P/BV Ratio Based Upon Peer Group Analysis

You are trying to estimate a price per share on an initial public offering of a company involved in environmental waste disposal. The company has a book value per share of $20 and earned $3.50 per share in the most recent time period. While it does not pay dividends, the capital expenditures per share were $2.50 higher than depreciation per share in the most recent period, and the firm uses no debt financing. Analysts project that earnings for the company will grow 25% a year for the next five years. You have data on other companies in the environment waste disposal business:

Company	Price	BV/Share	EPS	DPS	Beta	Exp. Growth
Air & Water	$9.60	$8.48	$0.40	$0.00	1.65	10.5%
Allwaste	$5.40	$3.10	$0.25	$0.00	1.10	18.5%
Browning Ferris	$29.00	$11.50	$1.45	$0.68	1.25	11.0%
Chemical Waste	$9.40	$3.75	$0.45	$0.15	1.15	2.5%
Groundwater	$15.00	$14.45	$0.65	$0.00	1.00	3.0%
Intn'l Tech.	$3.30	$3.35	$0.16	$0.00	1.10	11.0%
Ionics Inc.	$48.00	$31.00	$2.20	$0.00	1.00	14.5%
Laidlaw Inc.	$6.30	$5.85	$0.40	$0.12	1.15	8.5%
OHM Corp.	$16.00	$5.65	$0.60	$0.00	1.15	9.50%
Rollins	$5.10	$3.65	$0.05	$0.00	1.30	1.0%
Safety-Kleen	$14.00	$9.25	$0.80	$0.36	1.15	6.50%

The average debt/equity ratio of these firms is 20%, and the tax rate is 40%.

A. Estimate the average price/book value ratio for these comparable firms. Would you use this average P/BV ratio to price the initial public offering.

B. What subjective adjustments would you make to the price/book value ratio for this firm and why?

C. Using a multiple regression, specify the relationship between P/BV ratios and fundamentals in this peer group. What do the coefficients on the regression signify? How would you use the regression to make an estimate of the P/BV ratio for the IPO?

Question 8 - P/BV Ratios from Cross-sectional Regressions

Assume that you have done a regression of P/BV ratios for all firms on the New York Stock Exchange, and arrived at the following result:

P/BV = 0.88 + 0.82 PAYOUT + 7.79 GROWTH - 0.41 BETA
       + 13.81 ROE   {R^2=0.65}

where,

Payout = Dividend Payout Ratio During Most Recent Period

Beta   = Beta of the Stock in Most Current Period

Growth = Projected Growth Rate in Earnings Over Next Five Years

To illustrate, a firm with a payout ratio of 40%, a beta of 1.25, an ROE of 25% and an expected growth rate of 15%, would have had a price/book value ratio of

P/BV = 0.88 +0.82 (0.4) +7.79 (.15) - 0.41 (1.25)+ 13.81 (.25) = 5.3165

A. How could you use the R squared of the regression?

B. Consider the initial public offering in the previous example. Estimate the predicted P/BV ratio for this initial public offering using the cross-sectional regression. Why might this result differ from the peer group regression done in the prior problem?

CHAPTER 12

PRICE/SALES MULTIPLES

The price/earnings and price/book value multiples remain the most widely used of the multiples in valuation. In recent years, however, analysts have increasingly turned to value as a multiple of sales. This chapter describes some of the advantages associated with using this multiple, its determinants, and its use to examine the effects of corporate strategy and to assess the value of brand names.

Question 1 - Price/Sales Ratios: Concepts
Mark the following entries true or false.

A. Price/sales ratios can never fall below zero, whereas both price/earnings and price/book value ratios can be negative.

B. A firm with a high expected growth rate will sell for a higher price/sales ratio than a firm with a lower expected growth rate.

C. If profit margins come down, price/sales ratios will also decline.

D. A portfolio of stocks with low price/sales ratios is likely to contain a significant number of firms in businesses with low profit margins.

E. A strategy of investing in stocks with high profit margins is likely to yield excess returns.

Question 2 - Price/Sales Ratio for a Stable Firm
Longs Drug, a large U.S. drugstore chain operating primarily in Northern California, had sales per share of $122 in 1993, on which it reported earnings per share of $2.45 and paid a dividend per share of $1.12. The company is expected to grow 6% in the long term, and has a beta of 0.90. The current T.Bond rate is 7%.

A. Estimate the appropriate price/sales multiple for Longs Drug.

B. The stock is currently trading for $34 per share. Assuming the growth rate is estimated correctly, what would the profit margin need to be to justify this price per share.

Question 3 - P/S Ratio for an Industry

You are examining the wide differences in price/sales ratios that you can observe among firms in the retail store industry, and trying to come up with a rationale to explain these differences.

Company	Price	Per-Share Sales	Earnings	Expected Growth	Beta	Payout
Bombay Company	$38	$ 9.70	$0.68	29.00%	1.45	0 %
Bradlees	15	168.60	1.75	12.00%	1.15	34
Caldor	32	147.45	2.70	12.50%	1.55	0
Consolidated Store	21	23.00	0.95	26.50%	1.35	0
Dayton Hudson	73	272.90	4.65	12.50%	1.30	38
Federated	22	58.90	1.40	10.00%	1.45	0
Kmart	23	101.45	1.75	11.50%	1.30	59
Nordstrom	36	43.85	1.60	11.50%	1.45	20
Penney	54	81.05	3.50	10.50%	1.10	41
Sears	57	150.00	4.55	11.00%	1.35	36
Tiffany's	32	35.65	1.50	10.50%	1.50	19
Wal-Mart	30	29.35	1.05	18.50%	1.30	11
Woolworth	23	74.15	1.35	13.00%	1.25	65

A. There are two companies that sell for more than revenues: the Bombay Company and Wal-Mart. Why?

B. What is the variable that is most highly correlated with price-sales ratios?

C. Which of these companies is most likely to be over/undervalued? How did you arrive at this judgment?

Question 4 - Price/Sales Ratio for a High Growth Firm

Walgreen, a large retail drugstore chain in the United States, reported net income of $221 million in 1993 on revenues of $8298 million. It paid out 31% of its earnings as dividends, a payout ratio that is expected to remain level from 1994 to 1998, during which period earnings growth is expected to be 13.5%. After 1998, earnings growth is expected to decline to 6%, and the dividend payout ratio is expected to increase to 60%. The beta is 1.15 and this figure is expected to remain unchanged. The treasury bond rate is 7%.

A. Estimate the price/sales ratio for Walgreens, assuming its profit margin remains unchanged at 1993 levels.

B. How much of this price/sales ratio can be attributed to extraordinary growth?

Question 5 - Price/Sales Ratio and Changing Margins

Tambrands, a leading producer of tampons, reported a net income of $122 million on revenues of $684 million in 1992. Earnings growth was anticipated to be 11% over the next five years, after which it was expected to be 6%. The firm paid out 45% of its earnings as dividends in 1992, and this payout ratio was expected to increase to 60% during the stable period. The beta of the stock was 1.00.

During the course of 1993, erosion of brand loyalty and increasing competition for generic brands lead to a drop in net income to $100 million on revenues of $700 million. The sales/book value ratio was comparable to 1992 levels. (The treasury bond rate in 1992 and 1993 was 7%.)

A. Estimate the price/sales ratio, based upon 1992 profit margins and expected growth.

B. Estimate the price/sales ratio, based upon 1993 profit margins and expected growth. Assume that the extraordinary growth period remains 5 years, but that the growth rate will be affected by the lower margins.

Question 6 - Price/Sales Ratios and Brand Name Value

McDonald's Corporation, with fast food restaurants throughout the U.S, Canada and overseas, reported a net profit of $1.085 billion on sales of $7.425 billion in 1993. The sales/book value ratio in 1993 was approximately 1.2, and the dividend payout ratio was 20%. The book value per share was $19 in 1993. The firm is expected to maintain high growth for ten years, after which the growth is expected to drop to 6%, and the dividend payout ratio is expected to increase to 65%. The beta of the stock is 1.05. (The treasury bond rate is 7%.)

In contrast, Wendy's, a less well-known fast-food operator, reported a net profit of $90 million on revenues of $1475 million in 1993. It maintained a sales/book value ratio of 2.0 in 1993, and paid out 32% of its earnings as dividends. The book value per share was $7 in 1993. The high growth is expected to last for ten years, after which time it is expected to drop to 6%. The dividend payout ratio is expected to increase to 65%. The beta of this stock is also 1.05.

A. Estimate the price/sales ratio for McDonald's and Wendy's based upon their characteristics.

B. Assuming the McDonald's sales/book value ratio remains unchanged, estimate the price/sales ratio for McDonald's if its profit margin drops to that of Wendy's.

C. Assuming that the differences in profit margins between McDonald's and Wendy's are entirely attributable to differences in brand name value, estimate the value of the McDonald's brand name (relative to Wendy's).

Question 7 - Corporate Strategy and Profit Margins

Gillette Corporation, the leading producer of grooming aids, was faced with a significant corporate strategy decision early in 1994 on whether it would continue its high-margin strategy or shift to a lower margin to increase sales revenues in the face of intense generic competition. The two strategies being considered were as follows:

Status Quo High-Margin Strategy

* Maintain profit margins at 1993 levels from 1994 to 2003. (In 1993, net income was $575 million on revenues of $5750 million.)

* The sales/book value ratio, which was 3 in 1993, can then be expected to decline to 2.5 between 1994 and 2003.

Low-Margin Higher-Sales Strategy

* Reduce net profit margin to 8% from 1994 to 2003.

* The sales/book value ratio will then stay at 1993 levels from 1994 to 2003.

The book value per share at the end of 1993 is $9.75. The dividend payout ratio, which was 33% in 1993, is expected to remain unchanged from 1994 to 2003 under either strategy, as is the beta, which was 1.30 in 1993. (The treasury bond rate is 7%.)

After 2003, the earnings growth rate is expected to drop to 6%, and the dividend payout ratio is expected to be 60%, under either strategy. The beta will decline to 1.0.

A. Estimate the price/sales ratio under the status quo strategy.

B. Estimate the price/sales ratio under the low margin strategy.

C. Which strategy would you recommend and why.

D. How much would sales have to drop under the status quo strategy for the two strategies to be equivalent.

Question 8 - Price/Sales Ratio for a Peer Group

You have been asked to assess whether Walgreen Company is correctly priced relative to its competitors in the drugstore industry at the end of 1993. The following are the price/sales ratios, profit margins, and other relative details of the firms in the drugstore industry.

Company	P/S Ratio	Profit Margin	Payout	Expected Growth	Beta
Arbor Drugs	0.42	3.40%	18%	14.0%	1.05
Big B Inc.	0.30	1.90%	14%	23.5%	0.70
Drug Emporium	0.10	0.60%	0%	27.5%	0.90
Fay's Inc.	0.15	1.30%	37%	11.5%	0.90
Genovese	0.18	1.70%	26%	10.5%	0.80
Longs Drug	0.30	2.00%	46%	6.0%	0.90
Perry Drugs	0.12	1.30%	0%	12.5%	1.10
Rite Aid	0.33	3.20%	37%	10.5%	0.90
Walgreen	*0.60*	*2.70%*	*31%*	*13.5%*	*1.15*

A. Based entirely on a subjective analysis, do you think that Walgreen is overpriced because its price/sales ratio is the highest in the industry? If it is not, how would you rationalize its value?

B. Based upon a regression of the price/sales ratios of the comparable firms, what is your predicted price/sales ratio for Walgreen? What considerations would you have in using this regression?

C. Assume now that you are pricing an initial public offering of a private drugstore chain, which will offer personalized service at a much higher cost to wealthier individuals. The net profit margin is expected to be 6%, the firm is expected to pay out no dividends, and earnings are expected to grow 20% a year. The firm will have a debt ratio similar to the average firm in the industry. Estimate the appropriate price/sales ratio for this firm.

Question 9 - Price/Sales Ratio: A Cross-sectional Regression

You have regressed price/sales ratios against fundamentals for NYSE stocks in 1994 and come up with the following regression:

P/S = 0.42 + 0.33 PAYOUT + 0.73 GROWTH - 0.43 BETA +

7.91 MARGIN

For instance, a firm with a 35% payout, a 15% growth rate, a beta of 1.25 and a profit margin of 10% would have had a price/sales ratio of:

P/S   = 0.42 + 0.33 * 0.35 + 0.73 * 0.15 - 0.43 * 1.25 + 7.91 * 0.10

= 0.8985

A. What do the coefficients on this regression tell you about the independent variables relationship with the dependent variable? What statistical concerns might you have with this regression?

B. Estimate the price/sales ratios for all the drugstore chains described in question 7. Why might this answer be different from that obtained from the regression of only the drug store firms? Which one would you consider more reliable and why?

C. Price the initial public offering described in question 7, assuming that the revenues in 1993 were $250 million.

CHAPTER 13

MANAGEMENT DECISIONS, CORPORATE STRATEGY AND FIRM VALUE

The value of a firm is determined, in large part, by the decisions that it makes: in which assets to invest; in the appropriate leverage; and on how much to pay out as dividends. This chapter examines the relationship between corporate decisions and firm value, and provides a framework for evaluating the effects of restructuring on value.

Question 1 - Investment Decisons and NPV: Concepts

Evaluate, by designating as price up, price down, no effect or impossible to tell, the effects of the following investment decisions on stock prices:

A. A stable company with no growth opportunities takes a project with a NPV of $100 million.

B. A growth company (e.g., Microsoft) takes a project with an NPV of $100 million.

C. A company takes on a project with a NPV of negative $100 million.

D. A company announces an acquisition of a target firm for $500 million (the true value of the firm is only $350 million).

E. A company announces that it will be investing excess cash in treasury bonds.

Question 2 - Capital Structure: Concepts

Answer true or false to the following statements.

A. The value of the equity in a firm will increase as the firm takes on more debt.

B. The value of the firm will increase as it takes on more debt.

C. Debt increases firm value primarily because of the tax benefits it confers on the firm.

D. Debt is always cheaper than equity.

E. At the optimal debt ratio, the value of equity is maximized.

F. At the optimal debt ratio, the value of the firm is maximized.

Question 3 - Investment Decisions and NPV

Broderbund Software, a leading developer and publisher of educational software, was trading at $39 in March 1994, and there were 9.50 million shares outstanding. The company had no debt and reported earnings per share of $1.36 in 1993. The company paid no dividends and had a beta of 1.85. The treasury bond rate is 7.25%.

A. Estimate the proportion of the value attributable to future growth opportunities.

B. Assume now that Broderbund takes on a new project, which is expected to have an NPV of $10 million. Can you estimate the effect of value of this decision? Why or why not?

C. Would your answer change if Broderbund takes on a new project with an expected NPV of negative $10 million?

Question 4 - Acquisition Decisions and Stock Value

Novell Inc., which designs and manufactures high-performance local area networks, was trading at $23.75 per share on March 21, 1994. There were 308 million shares outstanding, and the firm had no debt. On March 22, 1994, Novell announced that it planned to acquire WordPerfect Corporation, a private company that produced and sold word processing software, for $1.4 billion. On the announcement, the stock price dropped $3.75 to $20 per share.

A. Estimate the value of equity at Novell, prior to the announcement of the acquisition.

B. Based upon the market reaction to the announcement, estimate the value that the market assigned to WordPerfect Corporation.

C. What other rationale could there be for the drop in Novell's stock price on the announcement of the acquisition?

Question 5 - Investment Decisions and Price/Book Value Ratios

Laidlaw Inc., a solid waste disposal company, had a decade of steadily declining return on equity starting in 1984 and continuing through 1993. The return on equity peaked at 16.2% in 1984 and dropped to 8% by 1993. Much of this decline could be attributed to projects that earned sub-standard returns. In early 1994, the price per share was $6.25, as was the book value per share. The firm paid out 40% of its earnings as dividends in 1993, and had a beta of 1.15. The treasury bond rate was 7.25%.

As part of a restructuring, the firm expects to choose better projects and improve its return on equity to 12%. The firm is in steady state.

A. Estimate the price/book value ratio assuming that the firm's return on equity remains at 1993 levels.

B. Estimate the improvement in the price/book value ratio assuming the firm manages to improve its return on equity to 12%.

C. Would it have made any difference if the projects that the firm takes to improve its return on equity were riskier than its past projects?

Question 6 - P/E Ratios and Franchise Opportunities

Lotus Development Corporation, a leading manufacturer of personal computer software, reported a return on equity of 14% in 1993 on a book value of equity of $540 million. The stock had a beta of 1.20 (the treasury bond rate is 7%). The company was expected, given current trends, to make a return on equity of 13.5% on future projects (which are expected to have a present value of $1 billion).

A. Estimate the price/earnings ratio for Lotus Development Corporation, given these inputs.

B. Estimate the price/earnings ratio for Lotus Development Corporation, if it improves its expected return on future projects to 16%.

Question 7 - Capital Structure and Firm Value

Arvin Industries, a major manufacturer of automotive emission and ride control systems, had earnings before interest and taxes of $130 million in 1993, and faced a tax rate of 40%. The firm had depreciation amounting to $76 million, and capital spending of $96 million in 1993. There are no anticipated working capital needs.

The firm is in steady state and is expected to grow 6% a year in the long term. The stock was trading at $31 per share in December 1993, and there were 22.2 million shares outstanding. The beta of the stock was 0.90. The debt outstanding was $435 million, and the firm had an A rating (leading to an interest rate on the debt of 8.25%). The treasury bond rate is 7%.

A. Estimate the current weighted average cost of capital for Arvin Industries.

B. Estimate the value of the firm, at its current capital structure.

C. Assume now that Arvin is planning to issue $100 million of stock and use it to pay down debt. This will raise the rating of the company to AA (leading to a drop in the interest rate paid on the debt to 7.75%).

Estimate the new firm value and value of the equity after this transaction.

D. If there were no default risk and interest tax savings are the only benefit of the borrowing, estimate the value of the firm at the old debt level and the new debt level. (You can assume that all debt is perpetual.)

Question 8 - Capital Structure: Empirical Evidence

There has been fairly substantial empirical evidence accumulated on the effects of changing capital structure. Which of the following statements reflects the findings in these studies?

A. Firms which borrow money increase their stock prices.

B. Firm which improve their bond rating increase their stock prices.

C. Firms which exchange one security for another increase their stock prices.

D. Firms which exchange one security for another, and decrease leverage in the process, increase their stock prices.

E. Firms which exchange one security for another, and increase leverage in the process, increase their stock prices.

Question 9 - Dividend Policy: Concepts

There are three schools of thought on dividends. The first school of thought argues that dividends are irrelevant and do not affect firm value. The second school of thought argues that dividends create a tax disadvantage and, therefore, decrease value. The third school of thought argues that investors like dividends, and that stock prices should therefore increase as dividends are increased. The empirical evidence is fairly ambiguous. Which of the following statements best summarizes these findings? (You can choose more than one.)

A. Dividends are sticky. Companies do not change dividends very often.

B. Just as many companies increase dividends as decrease them.

C. Companies that pay high dividends earn higher returns for their investors than companies that pay no dividends.

D. Companies that pay no dividends generally sell at very low prices.

E. When companies increase dividends, stock prices generally go up, and when they decrease dividends, stock prices generally go down.

Question 10 - Dividend Policy: Signaling Implication

The rationale that is often given for why stock prices go up on the announcement of dividend increases is that higher dividends send a positive signal about the future; companies that have better projects and expect higher cash flows will be much more likely to increase dividends than other companies, or so the story goes. Can you think of an equally viable story that would lead to the opposite conclusion (i.e., that higher dividends are a negative signal)? How would you test this hypothesis? Is the evidence consistent with this hypothesis?

Question 11 - Dividends and Firm Value

Long's Drug, a large drug store chain, paid dividends per share of $1.12 on earnings per share of $2.45 in 1993. The book value of equity in 1993 was $23.80 per share. The stock had a beta of 0.90, and the firm is in its stable growth phase. (The treasury bond rate is 7%.)

Walgreen Company, another drug store chain, paid dividends of $0.60 per share on earnings per share of $1.98 in 1993. The book value of equity was $11.55 in 1993. The stock had a beta of 1.15. The firm is in its high growth phase, which is expected to last five years, after which time the firm will be in its stable growth phase. (The return on equity is expected to drop to 13% in the stable growth phase.)

A. Estimate the value of Long's and Walgreen, based upon the current dividend policy.

B. Estimate the value of Long's and Walgreen if they increase their dividend payout to 60% of earnings.

C. Estimate the value of Long's and Walgreen if they decrease their dividend payout to 25% of earnings.

D. What broader lessons would you draw for dividend policy based upon this comparison?

Question 12 - Restructuring and Firm Value: Fundamentals

Black and Decker, a manufacturer of power tools, reported disappointing earnings per share of $0.65 in 1992 and $0.95 in 1993, down from $1.65 in 1988. The stock was trading at $21 per share, and there were 84 million shares outstanding (the book value of the equity was $1.12 billion at the end of 1993). The firm had accumulated $2.812 billion in debt (in both book and market value terms) by the end of 1993, on which it was paying almost 10.5% in interest. The high leverage caused the firm's beta to increase to 1.65. The firm is expected to pay out $0.40 per share in dividends in 1993. (The tax rate for the firm is 35%, and the treasury bond rate is 7%.)

The firm is considering a major restructuring, where it will attempt to do the following:

1. Improve its pre-tax return on assets to 1988 levels (which were 16%), by selling some overseas divisions and cutting costs at some domestic divisions.

2. Use the cash from the sale of assets (which is expected to be $1 billion) to pay down debt.

3. Reduce dividend payout by half.

These changes are expected to affect growth over the next five years, after which time growth is expected to be 6%, and the beta is expected to be 1.10, whether the firm restructures or not. (The dividend payout ratio will be adjusted accordingly.)

A. Estimate the value per share of Black and Decker assuming no restructuring.

B. Estimate the value per share of Black and Decker assuming the restructuring goes through.

Question 13 - Restructuring with Lower Costs

Intermet Corporation, an independent iron foundry organization, reported earnings before interest, taxes, and depreciation of $27 million on revenues of $450 million in 1993. The firm had $86 million in debt outstanding in 1993 (on which it paid 9% interest prior to taxes), and 25 million shares trading at $7.50 per share. The beta of the stock was 1.20. (The treasury bond rate is 7%.)

As a result of significant cost-cutting actions, Intermet expects to reduce its cost of goods sold (not counting depreciation) to 89% of revenues by the end of 1998 (five years from now). The cost reduction is expected to occur gradually over the next five years. Revenues are expected to grow 6% a year over the same period. Depreciation, which was $26 million in 1993, and capital spending, which was $38 million, are both expected to grow 6% a year from 1994 to 1998. Working capital is expected to remain 7.5% of revenues.

After 1998, the earnings and revenues are expected to grow 5% a year in perpetuity. Capital spending will be offset by depreciation. The debt ratio is expected to remain unchanged, but the pre-tax cost of debt is expected to drop to 8% by 1998. The tax rate is 40%.

A. Estimate the value of Intermet, as a firm and for the equity, assuming that the cost reductions are effective.

B. Estimate the value of Intermet, as a firm and for the equity, if the cost of goods sold declines to only 91% of revenues by 1998, rather than 89% of revenues.

CHAPTER 14

VALUATION FOR ACQUISITIONS AND TAKEOVERS

The process of valuation is central to acquisitions and takeovers. While all the theory discussed so far in this book applies to these valuations as well, there are unique situations in acquisitions that will receive specialized attention in this chapter. In particular, the questions of how to value synergy and corporate control will be examined.

Question 1 - Synergy: Conceptual Test

Answer true or false to the following statements.

A. If there is synergy, the value of the combined firm should be greater than the value of the companies operating independently.

B. Combining two firms, with volatile earnings, will increase value because earnings will become more stable after the merger.

C. When two firms merge, and do not use their additional borrowing capacity, there will be a transfer of wealth from stockholders to bondholders.

D. The empirical evidence suggests that merger gains are often overstated and fail to materialize in practice.

E. Firms generally become more profitable after mergers, relative to other firms in the industry.

Question 2 - Control Premium: Concepts

Answer true or false to the following questions.

A. The value of control is greater for a badly managed firm than for a well managed one.

B. Shares with restricted voting rights should sell for as much as shares with no voting right restrictions, if no one is attempting to take over the firm.

C. The empirical evidence suggests that the passage of anti-takeover amendments by a firm reduces its stock price.

D. Takeover restrictions passed by the state should not affect stock prices since all firms will be covered by these restrictions.

E. Hostile takeovers are bad for the economy because firms reduce investment, increase debt and sell assets after these takeovers.

Question 3 - The Value of Synergy: Cost Savings Example

The following are the details on two potential merger candidates, Northrop and Grumman, in 1993:

	Northrop	Grumman
Revenues	$4,400.00	$3,125.00
Cost of Goods Sold (w/o Depreciation)	87.50%	89.00%
Depreciation	$200.00	$74.00
Tax Rate	35.00%	35.00%
Working Capital	10% of Revenue	10% of Revenue
Market Value of Equity	$2,000.00	$1,300.00
Outstanding Debt	$160.00	$250.00

Both firms are in steady state and are expected to grow 5% a year in the long term. Capital spending is expected to be offset by depreciation. The beta for both firms is 1, and both firms are rated BBB, with an interest rate on their debt of 8.5%. (The treasury bond rate is 7%.)

As a result of the merger, the combined firm is expected to have a cost of goods sold of only 86% of total revenues. The combined firm does not plan to borrow additional debt.

A. Estimate the value of Grumman, operating independently.

B. Estimate the value of Northrop, operating independently.

C. Estimate the value of the combined firm, with no synergy.

D. Estimate the value of the combined firm, with synergy.

E. How much is the operating synergy worth?

Question 4 - Synergy Gains from Additional Debt Capacity

In the Grumman-Northrop example, described in the previous example, the combined firm did not take on additional debt after the acquisition. Assume that, as a result of the merger, the firm's optimal debt ratio increases to 20% of total capital from current levels. (At that level of debt, the combined firm will have an A rating, with an interest rate on its debt of 8%.) If it does not increase debt, the combined firm's rating will be A+ (with an interest rate of 7.75%.)

A. Estimate the value of the combined firm, if it stays at its existing debt ratio.

B. Estimate the value of the combined firm, if it moves to its optimal debt ratio.

C. Who gains this additional value if the firm moves to the optimal debt ratio?

Question 5 - The Value of Synergy: Higher Growth

In April 1994, Novell Inc. announced its plan to acquire WordPerfect Corporation for $1.4 billion. At the time of the acquisition, the relevant information on the two companies was as follows:

	Novell	WordPerfect
Revenues	$1,200.00	$600.00
Cost of Goods Sold (w/o Depreciation)	57.00%	75.00%
Depreciation	$42.00	$25.00

Tax Rate	35.00%	35.00%
Capital Spending	$75.00	$40.00
Working Capital (as % of Revenue)	40.00%	30.00%
Beta	1.45	1.25
Expected Growth Rate in Revenues/EBIT	25.00%	15.00%
Expected Period of High Growth	10 years	10 years
Growth rate After High-Growth Period	6.00%	6.00%
Beta After High-Growth period	1.10	1.10

Capital spending will be offset by depreciation after the high-growth period. Neither firm has any debt outstanding. The treasury bond rate is 7%.

A. Estimate the value of Novell, operating independently.

B. Estimate the value of WordPerfect, operating independently.

C. Estimate the value of the combined firm, with no synergy.

D. As a result of the merger, the combined firm is expected to grow 24% a year for the high-growth period. Estimate the value of the combined firm with the higher growth.

E. What is the synergy worth? What is the maximum price that Novell can pay for Wordperfect?

Question 6 - Tax Savings From Synergy

IH Corporation, a farm equipment manufacturer, has accumulated almost $2 billion in losses over the last seven years of operations, and is in danger of not being able to carry forward these losses. EG Corporation an extremely profitable financial service firm, which had $3 billion in taxable income in its most recent year, is considering acquiring IH Corporation. The tax authorities will allow EG Corporation to offset its taxable income with the carried-forward losses. The tax rate for EG Corporation is 40%, and the cost of capital is 12%.

A. Estimate the value of the tax savings that will occur as a consequence of the merger.

B. What is the value of the tax savings, if the tax authorities allow EG Corporation to spread the carried-forward losses over four years, i.e., allow $200 million of the carried forward losses to offset income each year for the next four years.

Question 7 - The Value of Control

You are considering a takeover of PMT Corporation, a firm that has significantly underperformed its peer group over the last five years, and wish to estimate the value of control. The data on PMT Corporation, the peer group, and the best managed firm in the group are given below:

	PMT Corp.	Peer Group	Best Managed
Return on Assets (After-tax)	8.00%	12.00%	18.00%
Dividend Payout Ratio	50.00%	30.00%	20.00%
Debt Equity Ratio	10.00%	50.00%	50.00%
Interest Rate on Debt	7.50%	8.00%	8.00%
Beta	Not Available	1.30	1.30

PMT Corporation reported earnings per share of $2.50 in the most recent time period and is expected to reach stable growth in five years, after which the growth rate is expected to be 6% for all firms in this group. The beta during the stable growth period is expected to be 1 for all firms. There are 100 million shares outstanding, and the treasury bond rate is 7%. (The tax rate is 40% for all firms.)

A. Value the equity in PMT Corporation, assuming that the current management continues in place.

B. Value the equity in PMT Corporation, assuming that it improves its performance to peer group levels.

C. Value the equity in PMT Corporation, assuming that it improves its performance to the level of the best managed firm in the group.

Question 8 - Analyzing a Leveraged Buyout

You are attempting to do a leveraged buyout of Boston Turkey, but have run into some roadblocks. You have some partially completed projected cash flow statements and need help to complete them.

Year	1	2	3
Revenues	$1,100,000	$1,210,000	$1,331,000
(Less) Expenses	$440,000	$484,000	$532,400
(Less) Deprec'n	$100,000	$110,000	$121,000
= EBIT	$560,000	$616,000	$677,600
(Less) Interest	$360,000	$324,000	$288,000
Taxable Income	$200,000	$292,000	$389,600
(Less) Tax	$80,000	$116,800	$155,840
= Net Income	$120,000	$175,200	$233,760

Year	4	5	Term. Year
Revenues	$1,464,100	$1,610,510	$1,707,141
(Less) Expenses	$585,640	$644,204	$682,856
(Less) Deprec'n	$133,100	$146,410	$155,195
= EBIT	$745,360	$819,896	$869,090
(Less) Interest	$252,000	$216,000	$180,000
Taxable Income	$493,360	$603,896	$689,090

(Less) Tax	$197,344	$241,558	$275,636
= Net Income	$296,016	$362,338	$413,454

The capital expenditures are expected to be $120,000 next year and grow at the same rate as revenues for the rest of the period. Working capital will be kept at 20% of revenues. (Revenues this year were $1,000,000.)

The leveraged buyout will be financed with a mix of $1,000,000 of equity and $3,000,000 of debt (at an interest rate of 12%). Part of the debt will be repaid by the end of year 5, and the debt remaining at the end of year 5 will remain on the books permanently.

A. Estimate the cash flows to equity and the firm for the next five years.

B. The cost of equity in year 1 has been computed. Compute the cost of equity each year for the rest of the period. (Use book value of equity for the calculation.)

Item	1
Equity	1,000,000
Debt	3,000,000
Debt/Equity Ratio	3
Beta	2.58
Cost of Equity	24.90%

C. Compute the terminal value of the firm and of the equity alone.

D. Evaluate whether the leveraged buyout makes sense from the viewpoint of equity investors, and in view of the entire deal.

CHAPTER 15

OPTION PRICING THEORY

Options are derivative securities, i.e., they are securities that derive their value from an underlying asset. Though traded options are of comparatively recent origin, option-like securities have existed for much longer. The technology available for valuing options has expanded dramatically in the last twenty-five years, especially since the development of the basic option pricing model by Black and Scholes. Their model, while setting the general framework for valuing options, has been modified to work in a variety of settings. An alternative model for option pricing, the binomial model, also provides more insight into the determinants of option value. This chapter examines the characteristics of options, the determinants of option value, and the basic option pricing model as a prelude to the application of these models to valuation.

Question 1 - Option Pricing: Conceptual Questions

Answer true or false to the following questions.

A. An option with less time to expiration will sell at a higher price than an option with more time to expiration. (Assume that the options are on the same stock and have the the same strike price.)

B. An option on a stock with higher variance will sell at a higher price than a similar option on a stock with lower variance.

C. An option can never sell for less than you can make by exercising the option.

D. A call option is always more valuable than a put option with the same strike price (with the same expiration on the same stock).

E. The payment of a dividend renders call options less valuable and put options more valuable.

F. A call option with a higher strike price can never sell for more than a call option with a lower strike price and the same expiration date.

G. Listed options will never be exercised early on a stock on which dividends are not paid.

H. As an option approaches expiration, its value will go down if the stock price does not change. (Assume that interest rates and the stock price variance do not change and dividends are not paid on the stock.)

I. The likelihood of early exercise on an option (on a stock which pays a dividend) increases as the time to expiration on the option decreases.

J. If a company's beta goes up, the options on the company's stock will become more valuable.

Question 2 - Binomial Option Pricing

The following is the binomial path for an underlying asset whose price currently is $50:

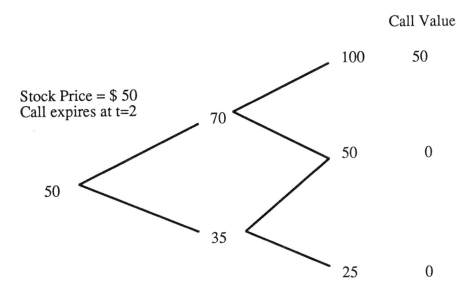

Call Value

Stock Price = $ 50
Call expires at t=2

The riskless interest rate is 10%.

A. Estimate the current value of a call with a strike price of 60 expiring at t=2.

B. Estimate the current value of a put with a strike price of 60 expiring at t=2.

C. Explain how you would replicate a call with a strike price of 60 at t=0? at t=1?

D. Explain how you would replicate a put with a strike price of 60 at t=0? at t=1?

Question 3 - Black-Scholes Valuation of Options on Non-Dividend Paying Stock

The following are prices of options traded on Microsoft Corporation, which pays no dividends.

	Call		Put	
	K=85	K=90	K=85	K=90
1 month	2.75	1.00	4.50	7.50
3 month	4.00	2.75	5.75	9.00
6 month	7.75	6.00	8.00	12.00

The stock is trading at $83, and the annualized riskless rate is 3.8%. The standard deviation in log stock prices (based upon historical data) is 30%.

A. Estimate the value of a three-month call, with a strike price of 85.

B. Using the inputs from the Black-Scholes model, specify how you would replicate this call.

C. What is the implied standard deviation in this call?

D. Assume now that you buy a call with a strike price of 85 and sell a call with a strike price of 90. Draw the payoff diagram on this position.

E. Using put-call parity, estimate the value of a three-month put with a strike price of 85.

Question 4 - Black-Scholes Valuation of Options on Dividend Paying Stock

You are trying to value three-month call and put options on Merck, with a strike price of 30. The stock is trading at $28.75, and expects to pay a quarterly dividend per share of $0.28 in two months. The annualized riskless interest rate is 3.6%, and the standard deviation in log stock prices is 20%.

A. Estimate the value of the call and put options, using the Black-Scholes.

B. What effect does the expected dividend payment have on call values? on put values? Why?

Question 5 - Dealing with Early Exercise

There is the possibility that the options on Merck, described above, could be exercised early.

A. Use the pseudo-American call option technique to determine whether this will affect the value of the call.

B. Why does the possibility of early exercise exist? What types of options are most likely to be exercised early?

Question 6 - Simple Option Replication

You have been provided the following information on a three-month call:

$$S = 95 \qquad K=90 \qquad t=0.25 \qquad r=0.04$$
$$N(d1) = 0.5750 \qquad N(d2) = 0.4500$$

A. If you wanted to replicate buying this call, how much money would you need to borrow?

B. If you wanted to replicate buying this call, how many shares of stock would you need to buy?

Question 7 - Valuing an Out-of-the-money Warrant: Small Number of Warrants Outstanding

Go Video, a manufacturer of video recorders, was trading at $4 per share in May 1994. There were 11 million shares outstanding. At the same time, it had 550,000 one-year warrants outstanding, with a strike price of $4.25. The stock has had a standard deviation (in log stock prices) of 60%. The stock does not pay a dividend. The riskless rate is 5%.

A. Estimate the value of the warrants, ignoring dilution.

B. Estimate the value of the warrants, allowing for dilution.

C. Why does dilution reduce the value of the warrants?

Question 8 - Valuing a Long-Term Option with Dividend Payments

You are trying to value a long term call option on the NYSE Composite Index, expiring in five years, with a strike price of 275. The index is currently at 250, and the annualized standard deviation in stock prices is 15%. The average dividend yield on the index is 3%, and is expected to remain unchanged over the next five years. The five-year treasury bond rate is 5%.

  A. Estimate the value of the long-term call option.

  B. Estimate the value a put option, with the same parameters.

  C. What are the implicit assumptions you are making when you use the Black-Scholes model to value this option? Which of these assumptions are likely to be violated? What are the consequences for your valuation?

Question 9 - Valuing a Long-Term Option with a Cap

A new security on AT&T will entitle the investor to all dividends on At&T over the next three years, limit upside potential to 20%, but also provide downside protection below 10%. AT&T stock is trading at $50, and three-year call and put options are traded on the exchange at the following prices:

	Call Options		Put Options	
K	1 year	3 year	1 year	3 year
45	$8.69	$13.34	$1.99	$3.55
50	$5.86	$10.89	$3.92	$5.40
55	$3.78	$8.82	$6.59	$7.63
60	$2.35	$7.11	$9.92	$10.23

How much would you be willing to pay for this security?

CHAPTER 16

APPLICATIONS OF OPTION PRICING THEORY TO VALUATION

Most readers of this chapter probably do not associate option pricing theory with equity or asset valuation. This chapter will aim to show that option pricing theory plays an important role in valuation, in that it provides a very different perspective that can be useful in understanding and analyzing high-technology firms, troubled firms and natural resource firms.

Question 1 - Valuing Equity as an Option: Concepts

Designate the following statements true or false.

A. Equity can be viewed as an option because equity investors have limited liability (limited to their equity investment in the firm).

B. Equity investors will sometimes take bad projects (with negative net present value) because they can add to the value of the firm.

C. Taking on a good project (with positive NPV) -- which is less risky than the average risk of the firm -- can negatively impact equity investors.

D. The value of equity in a firm is an increasing function of the duration of the debt in the firm (i.e., equity will be more valuable in a firm with longer term debt than an otherwise similar firm with short term debt).

E. In a merger, where two risky firms merge, and do not borrow more money, equity can become less valuable because existing debt will become less risky.

Question 2 - Valuing Equity as an Option: A Simple Example

XYZ Corporation has $500 million in zero-coupon debt outstanding, due in five years. The firm had earnings before interest and taxes of $40 million in the most recent year (the tax rate is 40%). These earnings are expected to grow 5% a year in perpetuity, and the firm paid no dividends. The firm had a cost of equity of 12% and a cost of capital of 10%. The annualized standard deviation in firm values of comparable firms is 12.5%. The five-year bond rate is 5%.

A. Estimate the value of the firm.

B. Estimate the value of equity, using an option pricing model.

C. Estimate the market value of debt and the appropriate interest rate on the debt.

Question 3 - Valuing Equity as an Option: McCaw Cellular

McCaw Cellular Communications reported earnings before interest and taxes of $850 million in 1993, and had a depreciation allowance of $400 million in that year (which was offset by capital spending of an equivalent amount). The earnings before interest and taxes are expected to grow 20% a year for the next five years, and 5% a year after that. The cost of capital is 10%. The firm has $10 billion in debt outstanding with the following characteristics:

Duration	Debt
1 year	$2 billion
2 years	$4 billion
5 years	$4 billion

The annualized standard deviation in the firm's stock price price is 35%, whereas the annualized standard deviation in the traded bonds is 15%. The correlation between stock and bond prices has been 0.5. The firm has a debt/equity ratio of 50%, and the after-tax cost of debt is 6%. (The beta of the stock is 1.50; the thirty-year treasury bond rate is 7%.) The three-year bond rate is 5%.

A. Estimate the value of the firm.

B. Estimate the value of the equity.

C. The stock was trading at $60, and there were 210 million shares outstanding in January 1994. Estimate the implied standard deviation in firm value.

D. Estimate the market value of the debt.

Question 4 - Valuing a Copper Mine

You are examining the financial viability of investing in some abandoned copper mines in Chile, which still have significant copper deposits in them. A geologist survey suggests that there might be 10 million pounds of copper in the mines still, and that the cost of opening up the mines will be $3 million (in present value dollars). The capacity output rate is 400,000 pounds a year, and the price of copper is expected to increase 4% a year. The Chilean Government is willing to grant a twenty-five year lease on the mine. The average production cost is expected to be 40 cents a pound, and the current price per pound of copper is 85 cents. (The production cost is expected to grow 3% a year, once initiated.) The annualized standard deviation in copper prices is 25%, and the twenty-five year bond rate is 7%.

A. Estimate the value of the mine using traditional capital budgeting techniques.

B. Estimate the value of the mine based upon an option pricing model.

C. How would you explain the difference between the two values?

Question 5 - Valuing an Oil Company Using Option Pricing Model

You have been asked to analyze the value of an oil company with substantial oil reserves. The estimated reserves amount to 10,000,000 barrels, and the estimated present value of the development cost for each barrel is $12. The current price of oil is $20 per barrel, and the average production cost is estimated to be $6 per barrel. The company has the rights to these reserves for the next twenty years, and the twenty year bond rate is 7%. The company also proposes to extract 4% of its reserves each year to meet cash flow needs. The annualized standard deviation in the price of the oil is 20%.

What is the value of this oil company?

Question 6 - Valuing a Project Using Option Pricing Model

You are analyzing a capital budgeting project. The project is expected to have a PV of cash inflows of $250 million and will cost $200 million (in present value dollars) initially. A simulation of the project cash flows yields a variance in present value of cash inflows of 0.04. You have to pay $12.5 million a year to retain the project rights for the next five years. The five-year treasury bond rate is 8%.

A. What is the value of project, based upon traditional NPV?

B. What is the value of the project as an option?

C. Why are the two values different? What factor (or factors) determine the magnitude of this difference?

Question 7 - Valuing a Company with a Product Patent

Cyclops Inc., a high technology company specializing in state-of-the-art visual technology, is considering going public. While the company has no revenues or profits yet on its products, it has a ten-year patent to a product that will enable contact lens users to obtain maintenance-free lens that will last for years. While the product is technically viable, it is exorbitantly expensive to manufacture, and its immediate potential market will be relatively small. (A cash flow analysis of the project suggests that the present value of the cash inflows on the project, if adopted now, would be $250 million, while the cost of the project will be $500 million.) The technology is rapidly evolving, and a simulation of alternative scenarios yields a wide range of present values, with an annualized standard deviation of 60%. To move toward this adoption, the company will have to continue to invest $10 million a year in research. The ten-year bond rate is 6%.

A. Estimate the value of this company.

B. How sensitive is this value estimate to the variance in project cash flows? What broader lessons would you draw from this analysis?

Question 8 - Valuing a Project As An Option: Concepts

Answer true or false to the following questions.

A. The right to pursue a project will not be valuable if there is a great deal of uncertainty about the viability of the project.

B. A project can be viewed as an option if and only if there are some barriers to entry which prevent competitors from replicating it.

C. A company which has valuable patents, which do not yet generate cash flows and earnings, will be undervalued using traditional discounted cash flow valuation.

D. A company should take on a project as soon as it becomes financially viable (i.e., when its NPV exceeds zero).

E. The value of a project will increase as the volatility of the industry and the technology underlying the project increases.

SOLUTIONS

A GUIDE TO USING THE SOLUTIONS

The following illustration is designed to explain the notation used in the solution manual.

Used in solutions	*Should be read as*
Revenues	Revenues
- Operating Expenses	(minus) Operating Expenses
- Depreciation	(minus) Depreciation
= EBIT	(results in) EBIT
- Interest Expenses	(minus) Interest Expenses
- Taxes	(minus) Taxes
= Net Income	(results in) Net Income
+ Depreciation	(plus) Depreciation
- Capital Expenditures	(minus) Capital Expenditures
- Δ Working Capital	(minus) Change in Working Capital
+ Net Debt Issues	(plus) Net Debt Issues
= FCFE	(results in) FCFE
+ Interest Expenses (1-t)	(plus) Interest Expenses (1 - tax rate)
- Net Debt Issues	(minus) Net Debt Issues
= FCFF	(results in) FCFF
FCFF * ∂	FCFF (multiplied by) Debt Ratio

CHAPTER 1 - SOLUTIONS
INTRODUCTION TO VALUATION

Question 1

D. Value is determined by investor perceptions, but it is also determined by the underlying earnings and cash flows. Perceptions must be based upon reality.

Question 2

E. Either A, B, or C.

Question 3

This statement is false. Qualitative factors such as quality of management and brand name value can (and should) be built into the analysis either in the profit margins or through the growth rate. Ultimately, the value of either should show up in cash flows and value.

Question 4

This statement is false. While biases affect all valuation, they can be factored in when the analyses are used. For instance, a valuation done by a positively-biased analyst should be scanned for overly optimistic assumptions about future growth/profitability.

Question 5

This statement is false. The value of any firm will also change as interest rates change, or as expected inflation changes. Values change both as a consequence of firm-specific information and market information.

Question 6

This statement is false. There may be more uncertainty about future prospects for the latter, resulting in a more imprecise estimate of value. This does not mean that the valuation is inferior.

Question 7

From the viewpoint of theory, the latter should work better. From the viewpoint of practice, there is a trade-off. The added inputs make the model more realistic and give it more depth, while the errors in coming up with these inputs may add to the error in the valuation. The net effect can be positive or negative.

Question 8

This statement is true, if the objective of the valuation is to pick undervalued and overvalued securities. However, there are other objectives in valuation: for purposes of examining the effects of corporate restructuring, or for private firm acquisition. Even a believer in market efficiency must use valuation models.

Question 9

First, the market must be inefficient, with undervalued and overvalued securities. Second, the dividend discount model must be the appropriate model to value stocks. Third, the inputs to the model must be estimated correctly. Finally, the market must correct itself within a reasonable period (Under and overvalued securities should become correctly valued).

Question 10

The valuation of a firm requires an understanding of the forces that drive success and failure in that industry. Your prior background in that industry may provide some insight into these forces. More importantly (and often left unsaid), your prior background may provide you with industry contacts who can be tapped for private information about competitive firms.

Question 11

For the most part, that is true. However, there are creative ways in which charts can be used in conjunction with valuation, to devise an investment strategy. For instance, valuation can be used for long-term investing, while technical analysis can be used to gauge short-term trends in prices.

Question 12

Only to a limited extent, and only if there is a relationship between how prices react to information and the degree of under- or overvaluation of the firm. Thus, if you can establish the fact that overvalued firms are likely to react more negatively to bad news, valuation can become a part of your strategy.

Question 13

This statement is false. Synergy and strategic considerations may be difficult to value, but they must be valued before an acceptable price is set.

Question 14

Good relations with analysts may help a firm smooth over misunderstandings, and get a hearing when bad news comes out, but it will not protect the company if it does not perform well (in terms of profitability and growth).

APPROACHES TO VALUATION

Question 1

A. False. The reverse is generally true.

B. True. The value of an asset is an increasing function of its cash flows.

C. True. The value of an asset is an increasing function of its life.

D. False. Generally, the greater the uncertainty, the lower is the value of an asset.

E. False. The present value effect will translate the value of an asset from infinite to finite terms.

Question 2

When equity is valued, the cash flows to equity investors are discounted at their cost (the cost of equity) to arrive at a present value, which is the value of the equity stake in the business.

When the firm is valued, the cash flows to all investors in the firm (including equity investors, lenders and preferred stockholders) are discounted at the weighted average cost of capital to arrive at a present value, which equals the value of the entire firm (generally much higher than the value of just the equity stake.)

The distinction matters for two reasons:

(1) Mismatching cash flows and discount rates can cause significant errors in valuation.

(2) Not recognizing what the present value of the cash flows measures can also lead to misinterpretations. For instance, if the present value of cash flows to the firm is treated as the value of equity, there is an obvious problem.

Question 3

A. PV of CF to Equity $= 250/1.12 + 262.50/1.12^2 + 275.63/1.12^3 + 289.41/1.12^4 + (303.88+3946.50)/1.12^5 = \$3224$

B. PV of CF to Firm $= 340/1.0994 + 357/1.0994^2 + 374.85/1.0994^3 + 393.59/1.0994^4 + (413.27+6000)/1.0994^5 = \$5149$

Question 4

A. It might be difficult to estimate how much of the success of the private firm is due to the owner's special skills and contacts.

B. Since the firm has no history of earnings and cash flow growth and, in fact, no potential for either in the near future, estimating near term cash flows may be impossible.

C. The firm's current earnings and cash flows may be depressed due to the recession. Other measures, such as debt-equity ratios and return on assets may also be affected.

D. Since discounted cash flow valuation requires positive cash flows some time in the near term, valuing troubled firms, which are likely to have negative cash flows in the foreseeable future, is likely to be difficult.

E. Restructuring alters the asset and liability mix of the firm, making it difficult to use historical data on earnings growth and cash flows on the firm.

F. Unutilized assets do not produce cash flows and hence do not show up in discounted cash flow valuation, unless they are considered separately.

Question 5

No. Any time a multiple is used, there is implicit, in that multiple, assumptions about growth, risk and payout. In fact, any multiple can be stated as an explicit function of these variables.

Question 6

A. Average P/E Ratio = 31.98

B. No. Eliminate the outliers, because they are likely to skew the average. The average P/E ratio without GET and King World is 25.16.

C. You are assuming that

(1) Paramount is similar to the average firm in the industry in terms of growth and risk.

(2) The marker is valuing communications firms correctly, on average.

CHAPTER 3 - SOLUTIONS
ESTIMATION OF DISCOUNT RATES
Question 1

A. It measures, on average, the premium earned by stocks over government securities. It is used as a measure of the expected risk premium in the future.

B. The geometric mean allows for compounding, while the arithmetic mean does not. The compounding effect, in conjunction with the variability of returns, will lower the geometric mean relative to the arithmetic mean.

C. The longer time period is most appropriate, because it covers more of the possible outcomes - crashes, booms, bull markets, bear markets. In contrast, a ten-year period can offer a slice of history that is not representative of all possible outcomes.

Question 2

Recent history is probably not an appropriate basis for estimating the premium, since this history can be skewed upward or downward by a couple of good or bad years. The premium should be based on the fundamentals driving the Malaysian market, relative to other emerging and developed markets, and estimate a premium accordingly. (Use 7.5% to 8.5% as the premium over the long-term bond rate.)

Question 3

CAPM: using T.Bill rate = 3.25% + 1.10 (8.41%) = 12.50%

CAPM: using T.Bond rate = 6.25% + 1.10 (5.50%) = 12.30%

The long-term bond rate should be used as the risk-free rate, because valuation is based upon a long time horizon.

* 8.41% is the arithmetic mean average premium earned by stocks over treasury bills between 1926 and 1990.

** 5.50% is the geometric mean average premium earned by stocks over treasury bonds between 1926 and 1990.

Question 4

An international portfolio manager would prefer a beta estimated relative to an international index. Daimler Benz returns would be regressed against returns on such an index to estimate its beta.

Question 5

A. Beta = 1.60 * 100/500 + 2.00 * 150/500 + 1.20 * 250/500 = 1.52

B. If they pay the cash out as a dividend: Beta = 1.60 * 100/350 + 1.20 * 250/350 = 1.31

If they keep the cash in the firm: Beta = 1.60*100/500 + 0*150/500 + 1.20*250/500 = 0.92

C. Use 2.00, the beta for the software division.

Question 6

A.

	Beta	D/E	Unlevered Beta
Weyerhauser	1.15	33.91%	0.95557808
Champion International	1.18	54.14%	0.89067359
Intenational Paper	1.05	45.50%	0.82482325
Kimberly-Clark	0.91	11.29%	0.85226741

The unlevered betas measure the business and operating leverage risk associated with each of these firms.

B. New beta for Kimberly Clark = 0.85 * (1 + (1-0.4) (0.30)) = 1.00

C. The average unlevered beta of these comparable firms should be relevered using the debt equity ratio of the initial public offering.

Average Unlevered Beta = 0.88

Beta of the Initial Public Offering = 0.88 (1 + (1-0.4) (0.40)) = 1.09

Question 7

A. CPC should have the highest beta (because of its high fixed costs) and Kellogg's should have the lowest beta (because of its low fixed costs).

B. Old Debt/Equity Ratio = D/(D+E)/(1 - D/(D+E)) = 0.3/ (1-0.3) = 0.4286

Unlevered Beta (using D/E ratio of 30%) = 0.88/(1 + (1 - 0.4) * 0.4286) = 0.70

New Debt/Equity Ratio = 0.7535/(1 - 0.7535) = 3.06

New Levered Beta = 0.70 (1 + (1 - 0.4) * (3.06)) = 1.985

Question 8

A.

Year	Earnings	∂ Earnings	Market Earnings Change
1988	$10.00		7.00%
1989	$15.00	50.00%	10.00%
1990	$18.00	20.00%	5.00%
1991	$18.50	2.78%	-10.00%
1992	$19.00	2.70%	-8.00%
1993	$22.00	15.79%	6.00%

∂ Earnings =   0.1716 + 1.8273 Market Earnings Change

The accounting beta is 1.8273.

B. The regression has only five observations, and earnings figures can be misleading.

Question 9

A. QVC/Paramount Beta = 1.05 * 6500/8500 + 1.70 * 2000/8500 = 1.20

B. QVC Unlevered Beta = 1.70/(1 + (1 - 0.35)(100/2000)) = 1.65
Paramount Unlevered Beta = 1.05/(1 + (1 - 0.35)(817/6500)) = 0.97
QVC/Paramount Unlevered Beta = 1.65 * 2100/(2100 + 7317) + 0.97* 7317/(2100 + 7317) =1.12
[Use values of the firm (debt + equity) as the weights for unlevered betas]
QVC/Paramount Levered Beta = 1.12 * (1+ (1 - 0.35) (7417/2000))
$$= 3.82$$
(New Debt = 817 + 100 + 6500 = 7417; New Equity = 2000)

C. Viacom/Paramount Beta = 1.05 * 6500/14000 + 1.15 * 7500/14000 = 1.10

D. Viacom Unlevered Beta = 1.15/(1 + (1 - 0.35)(2500/7500)) = 0.95
Paramount Unlevered Beta = 1.05/(1 + (1 - 0.35)(817/6500)) = 0.97
Viacom/Paramount Unlevered Beta = 0.95 * 10000/(10000 + 7317) + 0.97 * 7317/(10000 + 7317) = 0.958
Use values of the firm (debt + equity) as the weights for unlevered betas.
Viacom/Paramount Levered Beta = 0.958 * (1 + (1 - 0.35)(3317/14000))
$$= 1.11$$
(New Debt = 817 + 2500 = 3317)

Question 10

A. It measures the riskless rate during the period of the analysis.

B. There were four common economic factors driving stock returns over the estimation period.

C. The factor coefficients measure the risk premium relative to each factor, and the betas measure sensitivity to the factor.

D. Expected Return = 0.062 - 1.855 (-0.07) + 1.4450 (0.01) - 0.124 (0.02) - 2.744 (0.01) = 0.17638 or 17.638%

E. Expected Return = 6.25% + 1.05 * 5.50% = 12.025%

The CAPM assumes that the market factor captures all systematic risk. The APM allows for multiple sources of systematic risk.

Question 11

A. See second-to-last column below.

B. See last column below.

	Price	DPS	g	Beta	Cost of Equity DDM	Cost of Equity CAPM
Merck	$32.00	$1.06	15.00%	1.10	18.81%	12.30%
Ogden Co.	$25.00	$1.25	4.00%	1.30	9.20%	13.40%
Honda (ADR)	$25.00	$0.27	10.00%	0.75	11.19%	10.38%
Microsoft	$84.00	$0.00	NMF	1.30	NMF	13.40%

C. Use the CAPM estimate, because

(1) the DDM cost of equity cannot be calculated for many firms, with no dividends and/or no record of growth in the same; and

(2) the CAPM cost of equity has logical constraints. The DDM cost of equity does not.

Question 12

A.

	Market Value	Weights	Book Value	Weights
Debt	$2,000.00 m	5.24%	$1918	25.86%
Equity	$36,160.00 m	94.76%	$5500	74.14%

B. Cost of Equity = 6.25% + 1.10 * 5.50% = 12.30%

C. After-tax Cost of Debt = 6.45% (1 - 0.35) = 4.19%

D. Cost of Capital = 12.30% * (36160/38160) + 4.19% * (2000/38160)
= 11.87%

Question 13

A. Cost of Equity = 6.25% + 1.10 * 5.50% = 12.30%

B. After-tax Cost of Debt = 7.50% * (1 - 0.4) = 4.50%

C. Cost of Preferred Stock = 365/4000 = 9.125%

D. Cost of Capital = 12.30% * (710 * 55)/[(710 * 55)+ 65000 + 4000] +
4.50% * 65000/[(710 * 55) + 65000 + 4000] + 9.125% * 4000/[(710 *
55)+ 65000 + 4000] = 7.49%

ESTIMATION OF CASH FLOWS

Question 1

C. It is the cash that equity investors can take out of the firm after financing investment needed to sustain future growth.

Question 2

A. False. Capital expenditures may be greater than depreciation.

B. False. The dividends can exceed the free cash flow to equity.

C. True. The FCFF is a pre-debt cash flow. It can be equal to, but it cannot be lower than the FCFE.

D. False. The free cash flow to equity is after capital expenditures.

Question 3

A. False. It will result in too high a value.

B. True.

C. True.

D. False. There might be loss of value due to loss of depreciation tax benefits.

E. False. The discount rate also goes up.

Question 4

A. FCFE in 1992 = $41.10 + $12.50 - $15 - (175 - 180) = $43.60 million
FCFE in 1993 = $48 + $14 - $18 - (240 - 175) = - $21 million

B. Working Capital as Proportion of Revenues: 1992 = 175/544 = 32.17%
    Change in Revenues in 1993 = 620 - 544 = 76

FCFE in 1993   = $48 + $14 - $18 - (175/544) * (620 - 544)
                = $19.55 million

Question 5

A. $FCFE_{1992}$ = \$117.9 + \$573.5 - \$800 - (\$92 - \$34.8) + (2000-1750)

= \$84.20 million

$FCFE_{1993}$ = \$130 + \$580 - \$850 - (-370 - 92) + (2200 - 2000)

= \$522 million

B. $FCFF_{1992}$ = \$117.9 million + \$170 (1 - (652/770)) + \$573.5 - \$800

- (\$92 - \$34.8)

= - \$139.75 million

(The tax rate is extraordinarily high = 652/770; the taxable income is 770 million (940 - 170))

FCFF in 1993 = \$130 million + \$172 (1 - (670/800)) + \$580 - \$850 - (-370 - 92) = \$349.95 million

C. Debt Ratio = \$2200 million/(\$2200 million + 77 * \$29) = 49.63%

	1994 projection (in millions)
Net Income =	\$137.80
- (1 - 0.4963) * (850 - 580) * 1.06 =	\$144.16
FCFE =	-\$6.36

D. (Also in millions)

Net Income =	\$137.80
- (1 - 0.75) * (850 - 580) * 1.06 =	\$71.55
FCFE =	\$66.25

Question 6

	1991	*1992*	*1993*	*1994*	*1994* *(no debt)*
Revenues		\$8,494	\$9,000	\$9,360	\$9,360

- Operating Expenses	$6,424	$6,970	$7,249	$7,249
- Depreciation	$872	$860	$894	$894
= EBIT	$1,198	$1,170	$1,217	$1,217
- Interest Expenses	$510	$515	$536	$536
- Taxes	$362	$420	$437	$437
= Net Income	$326	$235	$244	$244
+ Depreciation	$872	$860	$894	$894
- Capital Expenditures	$950	$1,000	$1,040	$1,040
- Δ Working Capital	($235)	($5)	($0)	($0)
+ Net Debt Issues	($350)	($400)	$63	$0
=FCFE	$133	($300)	$162	$103
+ Interest Expenses (1-t)	$268	$330	$343	$343
- Net Debt Issues	($350)	($400)	$63	$0
=FCFF	$751	$430	$442	$442

Working Capital	$190	($45)	($50)	($50)	($50)
Total Debt	$5,750	$5,400	$5,000		
Debt Ratio				43.84%	

Tax Rate		52.62%	64.12%	64.12%	64.12%

Question 7

Year	FCFE/share	Terminal Value	Real CF
1	$1.12		$1.09
2	$1.25		$1.18
3	$1.40		$1.29
4	$1.57		$1.40
5	$1.76	$23.32	$21.63

Real Cash Flow = Nominal Cash Flow$_t$/$(1.03)^t$

A. Present Value = $1.12/1.14 + 1.25/1.14^2 + 1.40/1.14^3 + 1.57/1.14^4 +$ $(1.76 + 23.32)/1.14^5 = \$16.84$

B. Real Discount Rate = $1.14/1.03 - 1 = 10.68\%$

Present Value = $1.09/1.1068 + 1.18/1.1068^2 + 1.29/1.1068^3 +$ $1.40/1.1068^4 + (21.63)/1.1068^5 = \$16.84$

(Use real discount rates on real cash flows.)

Question 8

A. Expected Return = Expected Dividend Yield $*$ $(1 - 0.36)$ + Expected Price Appreciation $*$ $(1 - 0.25) = 0.0181 * 0.64 + 0.1119 * 0.75$
$$= 9.55\%$$

B.

	Before Taxes		After Taxes	
Year	Expected DPS	Terminal Price	Expected DPS	Terminal Price
1	$0.67		$0.43	
2	$0.75		$0.48	
3	$0.84		$0.54	
4	$0.94		$0.60	
5	$1.06	$62.79	$0.68	$56.34

Terminal price after taxes = $62.79 - (62.79 - 37.00) * 0.25 = \$56.34$.

C. Present Value = $\$0.43/1.0955 + \$0.48/1.0955^2 + \$0.54/1.0955^3 +$ $\$0.60/1.0955^4 + (\$0.68 + \$56.34)/1.0955^5 = \$37.76$

D. Present Value = $\$0.67/1.13 + \$0.75/1.13^2 + \$0.84/1.13^3 + \$0.94/1.13^4$ $+ (\$1.06 + \$62.79)/1.13^5 = \$36.99$

Question 9

A capital budgeting project generally has a finite life. Consequently it loses value over time. A stock has an infinite life. It generally increases in value over time, both as a consequence of inflation and real growth.

ESTIMATION OF GROWTH RATES

Question 1

Year	EPS	Growth rate
1987	$0.67	
1988	$0.77	14.93%
1989	$0.90	16.88%
1990	$1.10	22.22%
1991	$1.31	19.09%
1992	$1.51	15.27%

A. Arithmetic Average =   17.68%

B. Geometric Average =   17.65%

C. The geometric average considers the compounded effects of growth. The arithmetic average does not.

Question 2

A. Linear Regression =   EPS = 0.4413 + 0.172 (t)

   Growth rate from this regression model equals $0.172 a year.

B. Log-linear Regression =   EPS = -0.5841 + 0.1674 t

Growth rate from this regression model equals 16.74% a year.

C. Expected EPS next year using linear regression:

= 0.4413 + 0.172 (7) = $1.65

   Expected EPS next year using log-linear regression:

= Exp(-0.5841 + 0.1674 (t)) = $1.80

Question 3

Year	EPS	Corrected g	t
1987	7.27		1
1988	7.91	8.09%	2
1989	-0.97	-112.26%	3
1990	-2.64	172.16%	4
1991	8.42	131.35%	5
1992	-0.06	-100.71%	6
1993	10.75	100.56%	7

A. Geometric Average = (10.75/7.27)(1/6) -1 = 6.74%

B. Arithmetic Average Using Corrected Growth Rates =   33.20%

C. Linear Regression =   EPS = 3.8271 + 0.1389 (t)

  Expected Growth Rate = 0.1389/Average EPS =   3.17%

Question 4

A. Retention Ratio = 64%

   Return on Equity = 1625/5171 = 31.4%

   Expected Growth Rate = 0.64 * 31.4% = 20.10%

B. Growth Rate in 1993 = ($5,171 * (.25 -.314)/ $1,625) + 0.64 * 0.25

                 = -4.37%

C. Growth Rate After 1993 = 0.64 * 0.25 = 16%

Question 5

A. Retention Ratio = 1 - $660/$1080 = 0.3889

Return on Assets   = ($1080 + $550 * (1 - 0.4))/($6000 + $6880)

        = 10.95%

Debt/Equity Ratio = (6880/6000) = 1.14

Expected Growth Rate:

= 0.3889 (10.95% + 1.14 (10.95% - (550/6880) * (1 - 0.4)) = 7.00%

B. Retention Ratio = 50%

   Total Assets = $6000 + $6880 - $2500 = $10.380.

   New Return on Assets = (1020 + 550 * (1 - 0.4))/10380 = 13.01%

(The earnings before interest and taxes goes down by $100. The earnings after taxes will drop by $60. Note that interest expenses will be lower after debt is paid off, but the net income will go up by an equivalent amount.)

New Debt Equity Ratio = (4380/6000) = 0.73

New Expected Growth Rate

= 0.50 (13.01% + 0.73 (13.01% - 7%*(1 - 0.4)))

= 9.72%

C. Beta Before Change = 1.10

Unlevered Beta = 1.10/(1 + (6880/(330 * $63)) * (1 - 0.4)) = 0.9178

(Use market value of equity for this calculation)

Beta After Change   = 0.9178 * (1 + (4380/(330 * $63)) * (1 - 0.4))

        = 1.04

Question 6

A. Pre-Interest, After-Tax Profit Margin = EBIT (1-T)/Sales

        = 10 * (1 - 0.36)/ 60 = 10.67%

   Asset Turnover = Sales/Total Assets = 60/30 = 2

   Return On Assets = 0.1067 * 2 = 0.2134 Or 21.34%

   Retention Ratio = 35%

Expected Growth Rate

= 0.35 (0.2134 + 1 (0.2134 - 0.065 * 0.64)) =   13.48%

B. Pre-Interest, After-Tax Profit Margin = 9.00%

Return on Assets = 0.09 * 2 = 18%

New Growth Rate = 0.35 (0.18 + 1 (0.18 - 0.065 * 0.64))= 11.14%

C. Break-Even Asset Turnover = 0.2134/0.09 = 2.37

Question 7

A. Expected Growth Rate = 0.93 (25% + 0.10 (25% - 8.50% * (1 - 0.4))

= 25.10%

B. The following would be the expected changes :

(1) ROA will decline as the firm gets larger and the marginal projects are no longer as lucrative.

(2) Dividend payout ratio will increase.

(3) Debt/Equity ratio will increase as the firm gets larger and safer.

(4) The interest rate on debt will decline for the same reasons.

C. Expected Growth Rate = 0.5 (0.14 + 0.4 (0.14 - 0.07 * (1 - 0.4))

= 8.96%

Question 8

A. Weight analysts' forecasts the most, and historical growth rates the least (or not at all). In estimating growth rates from fundamentals, use predicted values for the fundamentals, rather than current values.

B. Use growth rates from fundamentals, and reflect the expected changes from the restructuring in these fundamentals.

C. Weight all three growth rates equally.

D. Use fundamentals on the remaining divisions to predict growth.

CHAPTER 6 - SOLUTIONS
DIVIDEND DISCOUNT MODELS

Question 1

A. False. The dividend discount model can still be used to value the dividends that the company will pay after the high growth eases.

B. False. It depends upon the assumptions made about expected future growth and risk.

C. False. This will be true only if the stock market falls more than merited by changes in the fundamentals (such as growth and cash flows).

D. True. Portfolios of stocks that are undervalued using the dividend discount model seem to earn excess returns over long time periods.

E. True. The model is biased towards these stocks because of its emphasis on dividends.

Question 2

A. A stock that pays no dividends is not a stable stock. The Gordon Growth model is not designed to value such a stock. If a company with stable growth insists on not paying dividends, but retains the FCFE, this FCFE can be used in the Gordon Growth model as the dividend.

B. A stable stock cannot have a growth rate greater than the discount rate, because no company can grow much faster than the economy in which it operates in the Gordon Growth Model. This upper limit on how high growth rates can go operates as a constraint in the model.

C. This should not happen for a stable stock, for the same reasons stated above.

D. It is true that the model smooths out growth rates in dividends. In present value terms, though, this smoothing effect cannot have a large effect on the value estimate obtained from the model.

E. The model requires that, in the long term, the growth rate for a firm is stable (close to the growth rate in the economy). Thus, cyclical firms, which maintain an average growth rate close to a stable rate, cyclical ups and downs notwithstanding, can be valued using this model.

Question 3

A. Cost of Equity = 6.25% + 0.90 * 5.5% = 11.20%
Value Per Share = $3.56 * 1.055/(.1120 - .055) = $65.89

B. $3.56 (1 + g)/(.1120 - g) = $80
Solving for g,
$$g = (80 * .112 - 3.56)/(80 + 3.56) = 6.46\%$$

Question 4

A. This should increase both the cost of equity (by raising interest rates) and the nominal growth rate. Whether the increase will be the same in both variables will depend in large part on whether an increase in inflation will adversely impact real economic growth.

B. This should affect the estimation of a stable growth rate. A much higher stable growth rate can be used for firms in economies which are growing rapidly.

C. An analyst has very limited flexibility when it comes to using the Gordon Growth model in estimating growth. If the growth potential of the industry in which the firm operates is very high, a growth rate slightly higher (1 to 2%) than the growth rate in the economy can be used as a stable growth rate. Alternatively, a two-stage or three-stage growth model can be used to value the stock.

D. Same as the answer to 3.

Question 5

A. Expected Earnings Per Share in 1999 = $2.10 * 1.15^5 * 1.06 = $4.48

Expected Dividends Per Share in 1999 = $4.48 * 0.65 = $2.91

Cost Of Equity After 1999 = 6.25% + 1.1 * 5.5% = 12.30%

Expected Price at the End of 1998 = Expected DPS in 1999/($k_{e, 1999}$ - g)
$$= \$2.91/(.1230 - .06) = \$46.19$$

B.

Year	EPS	DPS	
1994	$2.42	$0.79	
1995	$2.78	$0.91	
1996	$3.19	$1.05	
1997	$3.67	$1.21	
1998	$4.22	$1.39	$46.19
Cost of Equity = 6.25% + 1.40 * 5.5% =			13.95%
PV of Dividends and Terminal Price (@ 13.95%) =			$27.59

Question 6

A. Retention Ratio = 1 - Payout Ratio = 1 - 0.42/1.50 = 72%

Return on Assets

= (Net Income + Int Exp (1-t))/(BV of Debt + BV of Equity)

= (30 + 0.8 * (1 - 0.385))/(7.6 + 160) = 18.19%

Debt/Equity Ratio = 7.6/160 = .0475

Interest Rate on Debt = 0.8/7.6 = 10.53%

Expected Growth Rate

= 0.72 [.1819 + .0475 (.1819 - .1053 * (1 - 0.385))] = 13.5%

Alternatively, and much more simply,

Return on Equity = 30/160 = .1875

Expected Growth Rate = 0.72 * .1875 = 13.5%

B. Expected payout ratio after 1998:

= 1 - g/[ROA + D/E (ROA - i (1-t))]

= 1 - .06/(.125+.25(.125 - .07(1-.385))

= 0.5876

C. Beta in 1993 = 0.85

Unlevered Beta = 0.85/(1 + (1 - 0.385) * 0.05) = 0.8246

Beta After 1998 = 0.8246 * (1 + (1 - 0.385) * 0.25) = 0.95

D. Cost of Equity in 1999 = 7% + 0.95 * 5.5% = 12.23%

Expected Dividend in 1999

= ($1.50 * 1.135^5 * 1.06) * 0.5876 = $1.76

Expected Price at End of 1998 = $1.76/(.1223 - .06) = $28.25

E.

Year	EPS	DPS	
1994	$1.70	$0.48	
1995	$1.93	$0.54	
1996	$2.19	$0.61	
1997	$2.49	$0.70	
1998	$2.83	$0.79	$28.25

Cost of Equity = 7% + 0.85 * 5.5% = 11.68%

PV of Dividends and Terminal Price (@ 11.68%) = $18.47

F. Total Value per Share = $18.47

Value Per Share Using Gordon Growth Model

= $1.50 * 1.06 * 0.5876/(.1223 - .06) = $15.00

Value Per Share With No Growth = $1.50 * 0.5876/.1223 = $7.21

Value of Extraordinary Growth = $18.47 - $15.00 = $3.47

Value of Stable Growth = $15.00 - $7.21 = $7.79

Question 7

A. Cost of Equity = 6.25% + 0.85 * 5.5% = 10.93%

Value of Stable Growth = $0.48 * 1.07/(.1093 - .07) = $13.07

B. Value of Extraordinary Growth

= $0.48 * (6/2) * (.25 - .07)/(.1093 - .07) = $6.60

C. The payout ratio is assumed to remain unchanged as the growth rate changes. The payout ratio in this case is assumed to remain at 60% (0.48/0.80).

Question 8

A.

Period	EPS	DPS
1	$4.58	$0.79
2	$5.32	$0.92
3	$6.17	$1.07
4	$7.15	$1.21
5	$8.30	$1.43
6	$9.46	$2.35
7	$10.59	$3.56
8	$11.65	$4.94

| 9 | $12.58 | $6.44 |
| 10 | $13.34 | $8.00 |

B. Expected Price at End of 2003
   = ($13.34 * 1.06 * 0.60)/(.1175 - .06) = $147.54
   (Cost of Equity = 6.25% = 5.5% = 11.75%)

C.

PV of Dividends - High Growth =	$3.67
PV of Dividends - Transition =	$9.10
PV of Terminal Price =	$44.59
Value Per Share =	$57.36

CHAPTER 7 - SOLUTIONS

FREE CASH FLOW TO EQUITY DISCOUNT MODELS

Question 1

A. True. Dividends are generally smoothed out. Free cash flows to equity reflect the variability of the underlying earnings as well as the variability in capital expenditures.

B. False. Firms can have negative free cash flows to equity. Dividends cannot be less than zero.

C. False. Firms with high capital expenditures, relative to depreciation, may have lower FCFE than net income.

D. False. The free cash flow to equity can be negative for companies, which either have negative net income and/or high capital expenditures, relative to depreciation. This implies that new stock has to be issued.

Question 2

A. Value Per Share = $1.70 * 1.07/(.1203 - .07) = $36.20
(Cost of Equity = 6.25% + 1.05 * 5.50% = 12.03%)

B.

Current Earnings per share =			$3.20
- (1 - Desired Debt Fraction) *			
(Capital Spending - Depreciation) = 83.61%*		$1.00 =	$0.84
- (1 - Desired Debt Fraction) *			
Δ Working Capital	= 83.61% *	$0.00 =	$0.00
Free Cash Flow to Equity =			$2.36

Cost of Equity = 6.25% + 1.05 * 5.5% = 12.03%

Value Per Share = $2.36 * 1.07/(.1203 - .07) = $50.20

This is based upon the assumption that the current ratio of capital expenditures to depreciation is maintained in perpetuity.

C. The FCFE is greater than the dividends paid. The higher value from the model reflects the additional value from the cash accumulated in the firm. The FCFE value is more likely to reflect the true value.

Question 3

A.

Year	EPS	Cap Exp	Depr	ΔWC	FCFE	Term Price
1	$2.71	$2.60	$1.30	$0.05	$1.64	
2	$3.13	$3.00	$1.50	$0.05	$1.89	
3	$3.62	$3.47	$1.73	$0.05	$2.19	
4	$4.18	$4.00	$2.00	$0.06	$2.54	
5	$4.83	$4.62	$2.31	$0.06	$2.93	$84.74
6	$5.12	$4.90	$4.90	$0.04	$5.08	

The net capital expenditures (Cap Ex - Depreciation) and working capital change is offset partially by debt (20%). The balance comes from equity. For instance, in year 1:

FCFE = $2.71 - ($2.60 - $1.30) * (1 - 0.20) - $0.05 * (1 - 0.20) = $1.64

Cost of Equity = 6.5% + 1 * 5.5% = 12%

Terminal Value Per Share = $5.08/(.12 - .06) = $84.74

Present Value Per Share = $1.64/1.12 + $1.89/1.12^2 + $2.19/1.12^3 + $2.54/1.12^4 + ($2.93 + $84.74)/1.12^5 = $55.89

B.

Year	EPS	Cap Exp	Depr	ΔWC	FCFE	Term Price
1	$2.71	$2.60	$1.30	$0.05	$1.64	
2	$3.13	$3.00	$1.50	$0.05	$1.89	
3	$3.62	$3.47	$1.73	$0.05	$2.19	
4	$4.18	$4.00	$2.00	$0.06	$2.54	
5	$4.83	$4.62	$2.31	$0.06	$2.93	$52.09
6	$5.12	$4.90	$2.45	$0.04	$3.13	

Terminal Value Per Share = $3.13/(.12 - .06) = $52.09

Present Value Per Share = $1.64/1.12 + 1.89/1.12^2 + 2.19/1.12^3 + 2.54/1.12^4 + (2.93+52.09)/1.12^5 = 37.36

C.

Year	EPS	Cap Exp	Depr	ΔWC	FCFE	Term Price
1	$2.71	$2.60	$1.30	$0.05	$1.43	
2	$3.13	$3.00	$1.50	$0.05	$1.66	
3	$3.62	$3.47	$1.73	$0.05	$1.92	
4	$4.18	$4.00	$2.00	$0.06	$2.23	
5	$4.83	$4.62	$2.31	$0.06	$2.58	$45.85
6	$5.12	$4.90	$2.45	$0.04	$2.75	

Terminal Value Per Share = $2.75/(.12 - .06) = $45.85

Present Value Per Share = $1.43/1.12 + 1.66/1.12^2 + 1.92/1.12^3 + 2.23/1.12^4 + (2.58 + 45.85)/1.12^5 = 32.87

The beta will probably be lower because of lower leverage.

Question 4

A.

Year	EPS	Cap Ex	Deprec	ΔWC	FCFE	Term. Price
1	$2.30	$0.68	$0.33	$0.45	$1.57	
2	$2.63	$0.78	$0.37	$0.48	$1.82	
3	$2.99	$0.89	$0.42	$0.51	$2.11	
4	$3.41	$1.01	$0.48	$0.54	$2.45	
5	$3.89	$1.16	$0.55	$0.57	$2.83	$52.69
6	$4.16	$0.88	$0.59	$0.20	$3.71	

The net capital expenditures (Cap Ex - Depreciation) and working capital change is offset partially by debt (10%). The balance comes from equity. For instance, in year 1 -

FCFE = $2.30 - ($0.68 - $0.33) * (1 - 0.10) - $0.45 * (1 - 0.10) = $1.57)

B. Terminal Price = $3.71/ (.1305 - .07) = $52.69

C. Present Value Per Share = $1.57/1.136 + 1.82/1.136^2 + 2.11/1.136^3 + 2.45/1.136^4 + (2.83 + 52.69)/1.136^5 = \$35.05$

Question 5

A.

Year	1	2	3	4	5
Earnings	$0.66	$0.77	$0.90	$1.05	$1.23
(CapEx-Deprec'n) * (1-∂)	$0.05	$0.06	$0.07	$0.08	$0.10
Δ Working Capital * (1-∂)	$0.27	$0.31	$0.37	$0.43	$0.50
FCFE	$0.34	$0.39	$0.46	$0.54	$0.63
Present Value	$0.29	$0.30	$0.30	$0.31	$0.31

Transition Period (up to ten years)

Year	6	7	8	9	10
Growth Rate	14.60%	12.20%	9.80%	7.40%	5.00%
Cumulated Growth	14.60%	28.58%	41.18%	51.63%	59.21%
Earnings	$1.41	$1.58	$1.73	$1.86	$1.95
(CapEx-Deprec'n) * (1-∂)	$0.11	$0.13	$0.14	$0.15	$0.16
Δ Working Capital * (1-∂)	$0.45	$0.39	$0.30	$0.22	$0.13
FCFE	$0.84	$1.07	$1.29	$1.50	$1.67
Beta	1.38	1.31	1.24	1.17	1.10
Cost of Equity	14.59%	14.21%	13.82%	13.44%	13.05%
Present Value	$0.37	$0.41	$0.43	$0.44	$0.43
End-of-Life Index					1

Stable Growth Phase

Growth Rate: Stable Phase =	5.00%
FCFE in Terminal Year =	$1.92
Cost of Equity in Stable Phase =	13.05%
Price at the End of Growth Phase =	$23.79

PV of FCFE in High Growth Phase =	$1.51
Present Value of FCFE in Transition Phase =	$2.08
Present Value of Terminal Price =	$6.20
Value of the Stock =	$9.79

B.

Year	1	2	3	4	5
Earnings	$0.66	$0.77	$0.90	$1.05	$1.23
(CapEx-Deprec'n)* (1-∂)	$0.05	$0.06	$0.07	$0.08	$0.10
Δ Working Capital * (1-∂)	$0.27	$0.31	$0.37	$0.43	$0.50

FCFE	$0.34	$0.39	$0.46	$0.54	$0.63
Present Value	$0.29	$0.30	$0.30	$0.31	$0.31

Transition Period (up to ten years)

Year	6	7	8	9	10
Growth Rate	14.60%	12.20%	9.80%	7.40%	5.00%
Cumulated Growth	14.60%	28.58%	41.18%	51.63%	59.21%
Earnings	$1.41	$1.58	$1.73	$1.86	$1.95
(CapEx-Deprec'n)*(1-∂)	$0.11	$0.13	$0.14	$0.15	$0.16
Δ Working Capital *(1-∂)	$0.50	$0.48	$0.43	$0.36	$0.26
FCFE	$0.79	$0.97	$1.16	$1.35	$1.54
Beta	1.38	1.31	1.24	1.17	1.10
Cost of Equity	14.59%	14.21%	13.82%	13.44%	13.05%
Present Value	$0.34	$0.37	$0.39	$0.40	$0.40
End-of-Life Index					1

Stable Growth Phase

Growth Rate in Stable Phase =	5.00%
FCFE in Terminal Year =	$1.78
Cost of Equity in Stable Phase =	13.05%
Price at the End of Growth Phase =	$22.09

PV of FCFE in High Growth Phase =	$1.51
Present Value of FCFE in Transition Phase =	$1.90
Present Value of Terminal Price =	$5.76
Value of the Stock =	$9.17

C.

Year	1	2	3	4	5

Earnings	$0.66	$0.77	$0.90	$1.05	$1.23
(CapEx-Deprec'n) * (1-∂)	$0.05	$0.06	$0.07	$0.08	$0.10
Δ Working Capital * (1-∂)	$0.27	$0.31	$0.37	$0.43	$0.50
FCFE	$0.34	$0.39	$0.46	$0.54	$0.63
Present Value	$0.29	$0.30	$0.30	$0.31	$0.31

Transition Period (up to ten years)

Year	6	7	8	9	10
Growth Rate	14.60%	12.20%	9.80%	7.40%	5.00%
Cumulated Growth	14.60%	28.58%	41.18%	51.63%	59.21%
Earnings	$1.41	$1.58	$1.73	$1.86	$1.95
(CapEx-Deprec'n) * (1-∂)	$0.11	$0.13	$0.14	$0.15	$0.16
Δ Working Capital * (1-∂)	$0.45	$0.39	$0.30	$0.22	$0.13
FCFE	$0.84	$1.07	$1.29	$1.50	$1.67
Beta	1.45	1.45	1.45	1.45	1.45
Cost of Equity	14.98%	14.98%	14.98%	14.98%	14.98%
Present Value	$0.36	$0.40	$0.42	$0.43	$0.41
End-of-Life Index					1

Stable Growth Phase

Growth Rate in Stable Phase =	5.00%
FCFE in Terminal Year =	$1.92
Cost Of Equity in Stable Phase =	14.98%
Price at End of Growth Phase =	$19.19

PV of FCFE In High Growth Phase =	$1.51
Present Value of FCFE in Transition Phase =	$2.03
Present Value of Terminal Price =	$4.75
Value of the Stock =	$8.29

Question 6

A.

Year	1	2	3	4	5
Earnings	$1.02	$1.22	$1.47	$1.76	$2.12
(CapEx-Deprec'n)* (1-∂)	$0.00	$0.00	$0.00	$0.00	$0.00
Δ Working Capital * (1-∂)	$0.85	$1.02	$1.22	$1.47	$1.76
FCFE	$0.17	$0.20	$0.24	$0.29	$0.35
Present Value	$0.15	$0.16	$0.17	$0.18	$0.19

Transition Period (up to ten years)

Year	6	7	8
Growth Rate	15.00%	10.00%	5.00%
Cumulated Growth	15.00%	26.50%	32.83%
Earnings	$2.43	$2.68	$2.81
(CapEx-Deprec'n)*(1-∂)		$0.00	$0.00
Δ Working Capital *(1-∂)	$1.59	$1.22	$0.67
FCFE	$0.85	$1.46	$2.14
Beta	1.1	1.1	1.1
Cost of Equity	13.05%	13.05%	13.05%
Present Value	$0.41	$0.62	$0.80
End-of-Life Index		1	

Stable Growth Phase

Growth Rate in Stable Phase = 5.00%

FCFE in Terminal Year = $2.25

Cost of Equity in Stable Phase = 13.05%

Price at the End of Growth Phase = $27.92

PV of FCFE in High Growth Phase = $0.85

Present Value of FCFE in Transition Phase = $1.83

Present Value of Terminal Price = $10.46

Value of the Stock = $13.14

B. It is impossible to say. Easier credit terms will increase working capital as a percentage of revenues, and thus act as a drain on cash flows. On the other hand, the higher growth in revenues and earnings will create a positive effect. The net effect can be either positive or negative.

C.

Working Capital as % of Revenues	Value Per Share
60%	$8.62
50%	$10.88
40%	$13.14
30%	$15.40
20%	$17.66

* This assumes that there is no change in expected growth, as a consequence.

Question 7

A. Both models should have the same value, as long as a higher growth rate in earnings is used in the dividend discount model to reflect the growth created by the interest earned, and a lower beta to reflect the reduction in risk. The reality, however, is that most analysts will not make this adjustment, and the dividend discount model value will be lower than the FCFE model value.

B. The dividend discount model will overstate the true value, because it will not reflect the dilution that is inherent in the issue of new stock.

C. Both models should provide the same value.

D. Since acquisition, with the intent of diversifying, implies that the firm is paying too much (i.e., negative net present value), the dividend discount model will provide a lower value than the FCFE model.

E. If the firm is over-levered to begin with, and borrows more money, there will be a loss of value from the over-leverage. The FCFE model will reflect this lost value, and will thus provide a lower estimate of value than the dividend discount model.

CHAPTER 8 - SOLUTIONS

VALUING A FIRM - THE FCFF APPROACH

Question 1

A. False. It can be equal to the FCFE if the firm has no debt.

B. True.

C. False. It is pre-debt, but after-tax.

D. False. It is after-tax, but pre-debt.

E. False. The free cash flow to firm can be estimated directly from the earnings before interest and taxes.

Question 2

A. FCFF = **Net Income** + Interest (1-t) + Depreciation - Capital Spending - ΔWorking Capital

B. FCFF = (**Earnings before taxes** + Interest Expenses) (1 - tax rate) + Depreciation - Capital Spending - ΔWorking Capital

C. FCFF = **EBIT** (1- tax rate) + Depreciation - Capital Spending - Δ Working Capital

D. FCFF = (**EBITDA** - Depreciation) (1- tax rate) + Depreciation - Capital Spending - ΔWorking Capital

E. FCFF = (**NOI** - Non-operating Expenses) (1- tax rate) + Depreciation - Capital Spending - ΔWorking Capital

F. FCFF = **FCFE** + Interest Expenses (1 - tax rate) - New Debt Issues + Principal Repayments

* Assumed no preferred stock is outstanding.

Question 3

A. FCFF in 1993 = Net Income + Depreciation - Capital Expenditures - ΔWorking Capital + Interest Expenses (1 - tax rate)

= $770 + $960 - $1200 - 0 + $320 (1 - 0.36) = $734.80 million

B. EBIT   = Net Income/(1 - tax rate) + Interest Expenses

            = 770/0.64 + 320   = $1523.125 million

Return on Assets   = EBIT (1-t)/ (BV of Debt + BV of Equity)

            = 974.80/9000   = 10.83%

Expected Growth Rate in FCFF = Retention Ratio * ROA

               = 0.6 * 10.83%   = 6.50%

Cost of Equity = 7% + 1.05 * 5.5% = 12.775%

Cost of Capital = 8% (1 - 0.36) (4000/(4000 + 12000)) + 12.775%

            (12000/(4000 + 12000)) = 10.86%

Value of the Firm = 734.80/(.1086 - .065) = $16,853 millions

C. Value of Equity   = Value of Firm - Market Value of Debt

               = $16,853 - $4,000   = $12,853 millions

Value Per Share = $12,853/200 = $64.27

Question 4

A.

Yr	EBITDA	Deprec'n	EBIT	EBIT (1-t)	Cap Exp.	∂WC	FCFF	Term Value
0	$1,290	$400	$890	$534	$450	$82	$402	
1	$1,413	$438	$975	$585	$493	$90	$440	
2	$1,547	$480	$1,067	$640	$540	$98	$482	
3	$1,694	$525	$1,169	$701	$591	$108	$528	
4	$1,855	$575	$1,280	$768	$647	$118	$578	
5	$2,031	$630	$1,401	$841	$708	$129	$633	$14,941

	'93-97	After 1998
Cost of Equity =	13.05%	11.89%
AT Cost of Debt =	4.80%	4.50%
Cost of Capital =	9.37%	9.45%

Terminal Value

$= \{$EBIT $(1-t)(1+g) - ($Rev$_{1998} -$ Rev$_{1997}) *$ WC as % of Rev$\}/($WACC$-g)$

$= (841 * 1.04) - (13500 * 1.095^5 * 1.04 - 13500 * 1.095^5)$

$\qquad * 0.07 /(.0945-.04) = \$14,941$

Value of the Firm

$= 440/1.0937 + 482/1.0937^2 + 528/1.0937^3 + 578/1.0937^4 + (633 + 14941)/1.0937^5 = \$11,566$

B. Value of Equity in the Firm = ($11566 - Market Value of Debt) = 11566 - 3200 = 8366

Value Per Share = $8366/62 = $134.94

Question 5

A. Beta for the Health Division = 1.15

Cost of Equity = 7% + 1.15 * 5.5% = 13.33%

Cost of Capital = 13.33% * 0.80 + (7.5% * 0.6) * 0.2 = 11.56%

B.

Year	Deprec'n	EBIT	EBIT(1-t)	Cap Ex	FCFF	Term Val
0	$350	$560	$336	$420	$266	
1	$364	$594	$356	$437	$283	
2	$379	$629	$378	$454	$302	
3	$394	$667	$400	$472	$321	
4	$409	$707	$424	$491	$342	
5	$426	$749	$450	$511	$364	$5,014

	Now	After 5 years
Cost of Equity =	13.33%	13.33%
Cost of Debt =	4.50%	4.50%
Cost of Capital =	11.56%	11.56%

Value of the Division = $283/1.1156 + 302/1.1156^2 + 321/1.1156^3 + 342/1.1156^4 + (364 + 5014)/1.1156^5 = \$4,062$ millions

C. There might be potential for synergy, with an acquirer with related businesses. The health division at Kodak might also be mismanaged, creating the potential for additional value from better management.

Question 6

A. Cost of Equity = $7\% + 1.25 * 5.5\% = 13.88\%$

Current Debt Ratio = $1340/(1340 + 18.25 * 183.1) = 28.63\%$

After-tax Cost of Debt = $7.43\% (1 - 0.4) = 4.46\%$

Cost of Capital = $13.88\% (0.7137) + 4.46\% (0.2863) = 11.18\%$

B. & C. See table below.

D/(D+E)	Cost of Debt	Beta	Cost of Equity	AT Cost of Debt	Cost of Capital	Firm Value
0%	6.23%	1.01	12.54%	3.74%	12.54%	$2,604
10%	6.23%	1.07	12.91%	3.74%	11.99%	$2,763
20%	6.93%	1.16	13.37%	4.16%	11.53%	$2,912
30%	7.43%	1.27	13.97%	4.46%	11.11%	$3,063
40%	8.43%	1.41	14.76%	5.06%	10.88%	$3,153
50%	8.93%	1.61	15.87%	5.36%	10.61%	$3,265
60%	10.93%	1.91	17.53%	6.56%	10.95%	$3,125
70%	11.93%	2.42	20.30%	7.16%	11.10%	$3,067

80%   11.93% 3.43 25.84%   7.16%   10.89% $3,149

90%   13.43% 6.45 42.47%   8.06%   11.50% $2,923

Unlevered Beta = 1.25/(1 + 0.6 * (1340/(183.1 * 18.25)) = 1.01

Levered Beta at 10% D/(D+E) = 1.01 * (1 + 0.6 * (10/90)) = 1.07

FCFF to Firm Next Year = (637 - 235) * (1 - 0.4) * 1.03 = $248.43 million

Value of the Firm = 255.67 * 1.03/(WACC-.03)

Question 7

A. Cost of Equity = 7% + 2.2 * 5.5% = 19.10%

After-tax Cost of Debt = 10.31%(1 - 0.4) = 6.19%

Market Value of Equity = 45.99 * 9 = $413.91 million

Cost of Capital = 19.10% (413.91/(413.91 + 1180)) + 6.19% (1180/(413.91 + 1180)) = 9.54%

B. Unlevered Beta = 2.2/(1 + 0.6 * (1180/413.91)) = 0.81

New Beta = 0.81 (1 + 0.6 * 1) = 1.30

New Cost of Equity = 14.14%

After-tax Cost of Debt = 7.51%(1 - 0.6) = 4.51%

Cost of Capital = 14.14% (0.5) + 4.51% (0.5) = 9.32%

C.

Growth Rate	Old Value	New Value	Change
3%	$1,978	$2,046	$67
4%	$2,358	$2,453	$95
5%	$2,905	$3,050	$145

The value of the firm is calculated as follows:

FCFF in Current Year = 236 * (1 - 0.4) + 109 - 125 = $125.6 million

Value of the Firm Before the Change = 125.6 (1+g)/(.0954-g)
Value of the Firm After the Change = 125.6 (1+g)/(.0932-g)

SPECIAL CASES IN VALUATION

Question 1

A.

Year	EPS
1984	$0.69
1985	$0.71
1986	$0.90
1987	$1.00
1988	$0.76
1989	$0.68
1990	$0.09
1991	$0.16
1992	($0.07)
1993	($0.15)

Average Earnings Per Share = $0.48

Normalized Earnings Per Share in 1994 = $0.48 * 1.06 = $0.51

B.

Normalized Earnings Per Share =	$0.51
- (Cap Ex - Deprec'n) * (1 - Debt ratio) =	$0.25
- Δ Working Capital * (1- Debt ratio) =	$0.06
Normalized FCFE Next Year =	$0.19

(Assume that capital expenditures and depreciation will grow 6% in 1994.)

Question 2

A.

Total Assets in 1993 =	$25,000	(in millions)
Normalized Return on Assets =	12%	
Normalized Return on Assets (pre-tax) =	20%	

Normalized Income statement (based upon 12% ROA)

Earnings Before Interest and Taxes =	5000
Interest Expenses =	1400
Earnings Before Taxes =	3600
Taxes (at 40%) =	1440
Net Income =	2160
- (Cap Ex - Deprec'n) * (1-Debt ratio) =	500
FCFE	1660

Cost of Equity = 7% + 1.1 * 5.5% =	13.05%
Expected Growth Rate =	5%

Earnings before interest and taxes is calculated using the ROA:

ROA = EBIT (1- tax rate) / Total Assets = 12% (given in the problem)

Value of Equity = (1660 * 1.05)/(.1305 - .05) = $21,652

B. Value of Equity = $21,652/1.1305^2 = $16,942

Question 3

A.

Earnings Per Share Next Year =	$5.52
- (Cap Ex - Deprec'n) *(1- Debt ratio) =	$0.63
- (∂ Working Capital) * (1 - Debt ratio) =	$0.045
FCFE Next Year =	$4.845

Cost of Equity = 7% + 1.1 * 5.5% =   13.05%

Expected Growth Rate =   5.00%

Capital Expenditures - Depreciation = ($5.50 * 1.05 - $4.50 * 1.05)

Debt Ratio = 40%

Value Per Share = $4.85/(.1305 - .05) = $60.19

B. The value is very sensitive to assumptions about growth in 1993. If the earnings do not quadruple in 1993, the free cash flow to equity will be significantly below $4.85, and the value lower than $60.19.

Question 4

A.

Earnings Before Interest and Taxes =	$52.70
- Interest Expense =	$17.00
Earnings Before Taxes =	$35.70
- Taxes (40%)	$14.28
Earnings After Taxes =	$21.42
- (Cap Ex - Deprec'n) * (1-Debt Ratio) =	$3.75
- Δ Working Capital * (1- Debt Ratio) =	$4.76
FCFE =	$12.91

EBIT = Interest Expense * Interest Coverage Rate = $17 * 3.10 = $ 52.70
The change in working capital is based upon revenues growing at 4%.

B. Cost of Equity = 7% + 1.1 * 5.5% = 13.05%

Expected Growth Rate = 4%

Value of Equity = 12.91 * 1.04/(.1305 - .04) = $148.36 million

Question 5

A.

Year	Net Income	(in millions)
1987	$0.30	
1988	$11.50	
1989	($2.40)	
1990	$7.20	
1991	($4.60)	
1992	($1.90)	
Average =	$1.68	

Net Income =	$1.68
- (Cap Ex - Deprec'n) * (1 - Debt ratio) =	1.30
= FCFE =	$0.38

B. Cost of Equity (until 1996) = 7% + 1.2 * 5.5% = 13.6%

Cost of Equity (after 1996) = 7% + 5.5% = 12.5%

Year	Net Income	(Cap. Ex - Deprec'n) * (1 - Debt Ratio)	FCFE	Terminal Value
1993	$1.78	$1.37	$0.42	
1994	$1.89	$1.43	$0.45	
1995	$2.00	$1.50	$0.50	
1996	$2.12	$1.58	$0.54	$29.73
Term Year	$2.23	$0.00	$2.23	

Capital expenditures are offset by depreciation in the terminal year.

Terminal Value = $2.23/(.125 - .05) = $29.73

Value of Equity

$= 0.42/1.136 + 0.45/1.136^2 + 0.50/1.136^3 + (0.54 + 29.73)/1.136^4$

$= 19.24 million

Question 6

A.

EBIT (based upon operating margin of 12%) =	$1,440
Interest Expenses =	$340
Earnings Before Taxes =	$1,100
Taxes (at 40%) =	$440
Net Income (also FCFE)=	$660

Cost of Equity = 7% + 1.15 * 5.5% =	13.33%
Expected Growth Rate in FCFE =	6.00%

Value of Equity= (660 * 1.06)/ (.1333 - .06) =	$9,010

B. Value of Equity (assuming two year delay in return to profitability)
$= 9010/1.13325^2 = \$7{,}016$ million

Question 7

A.

	Equity	Debt
Market Value Weight	61.61%	38.39%
Cost of Component	13.33%	5.10%

Cost of Capital = 13.33% (0.6161) + 5.1% (0.3839) = 10.17%

B.

Year	1993	1994	1995	1996	Terminal Year
EBIT (1-t)	$8.25	$9.08	$9.98	$10.98	$11.42
- (Cap Ex - Deprec'n)	$0.00	$0.00	$0.00	$0.00	$0.00
- Δ Working Capital	$0.00	$0.00	$0.00	$0.00	$0.00
= FCFF	$8.25	$9.08	$9.98	$10.98	$11.42

Terminal Value $185.18

Terminal Value = $11.42/(.1017 - .04) = $185.18

Present Value = $8.25/1.1017 + $9.08/1.1017^2 + $9.98/1.1017^3 + ($10.98 + $185.18)/1.1017^4 = $155.60 million

C. Value of Equity = Value of Firm - Market Value of Debt = $155.60 - $109 = $46.60 million

Value of Equity Per Share = $46.60/15.9 = $2.93

Question 8

A. Unlevered Beta for Publicly Traded Firms in Same Business

$$= 1.30/(1 + 0.6 * 0.2) = 1.16$$

Debt/Equity Ratio for Private Firm

$$= \text{Debt/Estimated Market Value of Equity} = 10/30 = 33.33\%$$

New Levered Beta For Private Firm = 1.16 * (1 + 0.6 * .3333) = 1.39

New Cost Of Equity = 7% + 1.39 * 5.5% = 14.66%

B. Pre-Tax Cost of Debt = $1/$10 = 10%

After-Tax Cost of Debt = 10% (1 - 0.4) = 6%

Cost of Capital = 6% (0.25) + 14.66% (0.75) = 12.49%

C. *Using the Firm Approach:*

	1	2	3	4	5	Terminal year
EBIT	$2.40	$2.88	$3.46	$4.15	$4.98	$5.23
EBIT (1 - tax rate)	$1.44	$1.73	$2.07	$2.49	$2.99	$3.14
- (Cap Ex - Deprec'n)	$0.60	$0.72	$0.86	$1.04	$1.24	$0.00
= FCFF	$0.84	$1.01	$1.21	$1.45	$1.74	$3.14
Terminal Value					$41.85	

Terminal Value = $3.14/(.1249 - .05) = $41.85

Present Value (Value of Firm) (@ 12.49%) = $0.84/1.1249 +
$1.01/1.1249^2 + $1.21/1.1249^3 + $1.45/1.1249^4 + ($1.74 +
$41.85)/1.1249^5 = $27.50 million

Value of Equity = $27.50 million - $10 million = $17.50 million

Using the Equity approach:

	1	2	3	4	5	Terminal year
Net Income	$0.75	$0.94	$1.17	$1.46	$1.83	$1.98
- (Cap Ex - Deprec'n)						
* (1- Debt ratio) =	$0.45	$0.54	$0.65	$0.78	$0.93	$0.00
= FCFE	$0.30	$0.40	$0.52	$0.69	$0.90	$1.98
Terminal Value of Equity					$29.71	

Terminal Value of Equity = $1.98/(.1466 - .05) = $29.71

Present Value (using Cost of Equity of 14.66%) = $0.30/1.1466 +
$0.40/1.1466^2 + $0.52/1.1466^3 + $0.69/1.1466^4 + ($0.90 +
$29.71)/1.1466^5 = $16.76 million

Question 9

A. Unlevered Beta for Comparable Firms = 1.15/(1 + 0.6 * .25) = 1.00

Cost of Equity (until 1997) = 7% + 5.5% = 12.50%

Cost of Capital (until 1997) = 12.50%

Beta after 1997 for Boston Chicken = 1.15

Cost of Equity (after 1997) = 7% + 1.15 * 5.5% = 13.325%

Cost of Capital (after 1997)

= 13.325% (0.8) + 8% (1 - 0.4) (0.2) = 11.62%

B.

	1993	1994	1995	1996	1997
EBIT (1-t)	$9.72	$13.12	$17.71	$23.91	$32.29
Cap Ex - Deprec'n	$6.00	$7.20	$8.64	$10.37	$12.44
FCFF	$3.72	$5.92	$9.07	$13.55	$19.84

	1998	1999	2000	Terminal year
EBIT (1-t)	$37.13	$42.70	$49.10	$51.56
Cap Ex - Deprec'n	$0.00	$0.00	$0.00	$0.00
FCFF	$37.13	$42.70	$49.10	$51.56
Terminal Value			$778.80	

Terminal Value = $51.56 /(.1162 - .05) = $778.80 million

Present Value (using 12.50% for the first five years, and 11.62% after that) =$3.72/1.125 + $5.92/$1.125^2$ + $9.07/$1.125^3$ + $13.55/$1.125^4$ + $19.84/$1.125^5$ + $37.13/($1.125^5$ * 1.1162) + $42.70/($1.125^5$ * 1.1162^2) + ($49.10 + 778.80)/($1.125^5$ * 1.1162^3) = $401.67 million

This is both the value of the firm and the value of equity.

PRICE/EARNINGS RATIOS

Question 1

A.   Payout Ratio = 1.06/$2.40 = 44.17 %

Expected Growth Rate = 6%

Cost of Equity = 7% + 1.05 * 5.5% = 12.775%

P/E Ratio = 0.4417 * 1.06/(.12775 - .06) = 6.91

B.   The stock is trading at ten times earnings.

P/E Ratio = 10 = 0.4417 (1+g)/(.12775-g)

Solving for g in this equation,

g   = (1.2775 - 0.4417)/10.4417 = 8.00%

Question 2

A. Dividend Payout Ratio   = Dividend Yield/(1/P/E)

= 0.025/(1/16.9)   = 0.4225

Expected Growth Rate

= (1+Real Growth Rate) (1+ Expected Inflation) - 1

= 1.035 * 1.025 -1 = 6.09%

Cost of Equity = 6.95% + 5.5% = 12.45%

Expected P/E Ratio   = Payout * (1 + g)/(r - g)

= 0.4225 * 1.0609/(.1245 - .0609) = 7.05

B. P/E Ratio = 16.9 = 0.4225 (1+g)/(.1245 - g)

Solving for g,

g = (16.9 * .1245 - 0.4225)/(16.9 + 0.4225) = 9.71%

C. Yes. It has to be real growth. If the growth arises because of higher inflation, interest rates will also rise, erasing much of the benefits of higher growth.

Question 3

A.

	First 5 Years	After Year 5
Dividend Payout Ratio =	55.49%	60.00%
Return On Equity =	20.00%	15.00%
Expected Growth Rate =	8.90%	6.00%
Cost Of Equity =	13.05%	13.05%

$$PE = \frac{0.5549 * (1.0890) * \left(1 - \frac{(1.0890)^5}{(1.1305)^5}\right)}{(.1305 - .0890)} + \frac{0.6 * (1.089)^5 * (1.06)}{(.1305 - .06)(1.1305)^5}$$

$$= 9.97$$

B. P/E Ratio Based Upon Stable Growth (6%; 60% dividend payout)
= 0.6 * 1.06/(.1305 - .06) = 9.02
Difference Due to High Growth = 9.97 - 9.02 = 0.95

Question 4

A. $$PE = \frac{0.10 * (1.15) * \left(1 - \frac{(1.15)^5}{(1.1388)^5}\right)}{(.1388 - .15)} + \frac{0.5 * (1.15)^5 * (1.06)}{(.1305 - .06)(1.1388)^5}$$

$$= 8.41$$

B. Growth Rate from 1983 to 1993 = $(0.78/0.08)^{(1/10)} - 1 = 25.57\%$

$$PE = \frac{0.10 * (1.2557) * \left(1 - \frac{(1.2557)^5}{(1.1388)^5}\right)}{(.1388 - .2557)} + \frac{0.5 * (1.2557)^5 * (1.06)}{(.1305 - .06)(1.1388)^5}$$

$$= 12.94$$

$$C. \quad PE = \frac{0.10 * (1.10) * \left(1 - \frac{(1.10)^5}{(1.1388)^5}\right)}{(.1388 - .10)} + \frac{0.5 * (1.10)^5 * (1.06)}{(.1305 - .06)(1.1388)^5} = 6.77$$

Question 5

A.	*South Korea*	*Thailand*
Dividend Payout	60%	60%
Expected Growth	(1.065)(1.058) - 1	(1.075)(1.049) - 1
	= 12.68%	= 12.77%
Cost of Equity	12.90% + 7.5%	8.00% + 7.50%
	= 20.40%	= 15.50%
P/E Ratio	0.6 * 1.1268/	0.6 * 1.1277/
	(.204 - .1268)	(.1550 - .1277)
	= 8.75	= 24.76

*Expected Growth (in Nominal terms)
= (1+Expected Real Growth) (1+Exp. Inflation)

B. The regression yields the following:

P/E = 28.765 + 16.732 Interest Rate - 102.8 Inflation + 24.57 GDP
    Growth

$R^2 = 0.4175$

C.

Emerging Market	P/E Ratio	Predicted P/E	P/E -Predicted
China	18.0	16.99768	1.00

Hong Kong	18.1	24.46113	-6.36
India	26.6	22.41671	4.18
Indonesia	24.1	23.22113	0.88
Malaysia	34.6	28.26511	6.33
Philippines	21.5	22.43933	-0.94
Singapore	26.2	29.01850	-2.82
South Korea	22.0	26.56018	-4.56
Taiwan	34.0	28.30933	5.69
Thailand	23.5	26.91087	-3.41

Negative numbers suggest the market is undervalued. Positive numbers suggest overvaluation.

Question 6

A.   Dividend Payout Ratio = 0.0274/(1/21.2) = 0.581
        Cost of Equity = 6% + 5.5% = 11.5%

Solving for the Implied Growth Rate
        g = (21.2 * .115 - 0.581)/(21.2 + .581) = 8.53%
        1+g = (1+ Expected Inflation Rate) (1+ Real Growth Rate)

Solving for Expected Inflation
        1.0853 = (1+Expected Inflation rate) (1.025)
        Expected Inflation Rate = 1.0853/1.025 - 1 = 5.88%

B. The P/E ratio would go down. For instance, in the formulation above,
        Dividend Payout Ratio = 0.581
        Cost of Equity = 12.5%
        Expected Growth Rate =8.53%
The new P/E ratio would be

P/E = 0.581 (1.0853)/(.125 - .0853) = 15.88

C. Not necessarily. If the increase in expected real growth is greater than the increase in interest rates, P/E ratios may go up as interest rates go up.

Question 7

A.   Average P/E Ratio for the Industry = 13.2

        Median P/E Ratio for the Industry = 12.25

If the firms in this group are homogeneous, the average P/E ratio provides an estimate of how much the market values earnings in this sector, given the expected growth potential and the risk in the sector.

        The average P/E ratio can be skewed by extreme values (usually high, since P/E cannot be less than zero). The median corrects for this by looking at the median firm in the sector.

B. This statement is likely to be true only if

(1) Thiokol has the same growth prospects and risk profile of the typical firm in the industry. It also generates cash flows for disbursement as dividends which are similar to the typical firm in the industry.

(2) Thiokol has higher growth potential and/or lower risk than the typical firm in the industry.

C. The regression of P/E ratios on fundamentals yields the following:

P/E = -2.33 + 35.74 Growth Rate + 11.97 Beta + 2.90 Payout Ratio

$$R^2 = 0.4068$$

The following table provides predicted P/E ratios for the firms in the group:

	Actual P/E	Predicted P/E	Difference
Boeing	17.30	12.90	4.40
General Dynamics	15.50	17.90	-2.40
GM- Hughes	16.50	13.68	2.82
Grumman	11.40	12.07	-0.67
Lockheed Corp.	10.20	12.31	-2.11
Logicon	12.40	13.17	-0.77
Loral Corporation	13.30	13.21	0.09
Martin Marietta	11.00	11.34	-0.34
McDonnell Doug.	22.60	17.15	5.45
Northrop	9.50	14.82	-5.32
Raytheon	12.10	10.85	1.25
Rockwell	13.90	14.85	-0.95
Thiokol	8.70	11.44	-2.74
United Industrial	10.40	9.11	1.29

Again, negative numbers indicate that the stock is undervalued.

The problem with a regression like this one is that it has relatively few observations and is likely to be thrown off by a few extreme observations.

Question 8

A. Expected Growth Rate = 25%

Unlevered Beta = $1.15/(1 + 0.6 * 0.25) = 1.00$

FCFE = Net Income + Depreciation - Capital Spending = $10 + 5 - 12 = 3$

Estimated Dividend Payout Ratio = $3/10 = 30\%$

P/E = $18.69 + 0.0695 * 25 - 0.5082 (1.00) - 0.4262 * 0.30 = 19.79$

B.

1. The cross-sectional relationship between P/E ratio and the fundamentals may change over time.

2. The market might be overvaluing all stocks.

3. Some of the fundamentals, such as growth rate or beta, might be estimated with error.

Question 9

F. A firm with a lower P/E ratio than its peer group, a higher expected
  growth rate and lower risk.

Question 10

A. Expected Growth Rate = 10%

  Cost of Equity = 7% + 0.8 * 5.5% = 11.4%

  FCFE = Net Income + (Cap Ex - Depreciation) (1 - debt ratio)
      + Working Capital Change (1- Debt ratio)
      = 120 - (80 - 77) * .9 - 15 * .9 = \$103.8 million

$$\frac{P_0}{FCFE_0} = \frac{(1.10)\left(1 - \frac{(1.10)^5}{(1.114)^5}\right)}{.114-.10} + \frac{(1.10)^5(1.06)}{(.114-.06)(1.114)^5} = 23.24$$

B. EBIT   = Net Income/(1-tax rate)+Interest Expenses
      = 120/0.6 + 19 = \$219 million

FCFF = 219 * (1 - 0.4) - (80 - 77) - 15 = 113.4 million

Value of Firm = Value of Equity + Value of Debt
      = 23.24 * 103.8 + 251 = \$2663 million

Value of Firm/FCFF = 2663/113.4 = 23.48

Value of Firm/EBIT = 2663/219 = 12.16 (lower because it is a pre-tax number)

Value of firm/EBITDA = 2663/(219+77) = 9.00 (lower because depreciation is added in while capital expenditures are ignored)

PRICE/BOOK VALUE MULTIPLES

Question 1

A. False. If the ROE< Required rate of return, this can be justified.

B. False, since the drop can be temporary. If the drop is permanent, this will be generally true, since there will be a two-layered impact. The growth will go down, pushing down Price/Book value ratios. The ROE will also go down pushing P/BV ratios down even further.

C. True.

D. True. If other things (like risk) are not equal, this can be false.

E. False. The growth rate will be lower for these firms. The net effect may be a lower price/book value ratio.

Question 2

A.   Dividend Payout Ratio = $2/$4 = 50%

       Return on Equity = $4/$40 = 10%

       Cost of Equity = 7% +0.85 * 5.5% = 11.68%

       Expected Growth Rate = 6%

       Price/Book Value Ratio = (.1) (.5)(1.06)/(.1168 - .06) = 0.93

A simpler solution might be the following:

       Price/Book Value Ratio = (.10 - .06)/(.1168 - .06) = 0.70

(This solution takes into account the relationship between ROE and g, i.e., g=b(ROE))

B.   If the P/BV ratio is 1.5, using the first approach,

       1.5 = ROE (.5) (1.06)/(.1168 - .06),

       Solving for ROE = 16.08%

       Using the second approach,

$1.5 = (ROE - .06)/(.1168 - .06)$

Solving for ROE = 14.52%

Question 3

A. Average Price/Book Value Ratio = 2.28

Average ROE = 12.44%

Average Beta = 1.10

B. Cost of Equity (based upon average beta) $= 7\% + 1.1 * 5.5\%$

$$= 13.05\%$$

If $P/BV = (ROE - g)/(r - g)$,

and ROE < r, (as in this case)

then P/BV <1.

Therefore, one may conclude that stocks in the industry are, on average, overvalued relative to book value (assuming that the industry overall is in stable growth, although individual firms might still have extraordinary growth).

Question 4

A.

Price / Book Value of Equity

$$= \left[0.21 * \frac{0.10 * (1.30) * \left(1 - \frac{(1.30)^5}{(1.1633)^5} \right)}{(.1633 - .30)} + 0.21 * \frac{0.60 * (1.30)^5 * (1.06)}{(.133 - .06) (1.1633)^5} \right]$$

$$= 3.34$$

B.

Growth Rate	Price/Book Value Ratio
10%	1.47
15%	1.83
20%	2.25
25%	2.75
30%	3.34
40%	4.81
50%	6.76

C. Between 11 and 12 years (this can be solved through trial and error).

Question 5

A.

	Next 10 yrs	After yr 10
Payout Ratio	37.00%	60.00%
Expected Growth	19.85%	6.00%
Cost of Equity	12.88%	11.50%
ROE	31.50%	15.00%

Expected Growth Rate = (1 - Payout Ratio)*ROE = (1 - .37) (.3150)

$$= .1985$$

Payout Ratio After Year 10   = 1 - Growth Rate / ROE

$$= 1 - 6\%/15\% = .60$$

Price / Book Value of Equity

$$= \left[0.315 * \frac{0.37 * (1.1985) * \left(1 - \frac{(1.1985)^{10}}{(1.1288)^{10}} \right)}{(.1288 - .1985)} + 0.15 * \frac{0.60 * (1.1985)^{10} * (1.06)}{(.115 - .06) (1.1288)^{10}} \right]$$

$$= 4.80$$

B.

	Next 10 years	After year 10
Payout Ratio	37.00%	60.00%
Expected Growth	12.60%	6.00%
Cost of Equity	12.88%	11.50%
ROE	20.00%	15.00%

Expected Growth Rate = (1 - Payout Ratio)*ROE = (1 - .37) (.20)

$$= .126$$

$$PBV = \left[0.20 * \frac{0.37 * (1.126) * \left(1 - \frac{(1.126)^{10}}{(1.1288)^{10}} \right)}{(.1288 - .126)} + 0.15 * \frac{0.60 * (1.126)^{10} * (1.06)}{(.115 - .06) (1.1288)^{10}} \right]$$

$$= 2.42$$

Question 6

A.

Year   ROE   g = b (ROE) Period of Growth P/BV

1988	27.00%	27.00%	10	2.55
1989	26.30%	26.30%	9	2.17
1990	23.90%	23.90%	8	1.68
1991	21.50%	21.50%	7	1.34
1992	18.30%	18.30%	6	1.07
1993	6.30%	6.30%	5	0.60

The price/book value ratio is estimated using a growth rate of 6% and a payout ratio of 50% after the period of high growth. The cost of equity used in the discounting is 13.6%.

B. No. The P/BV ratios are based upon expected returns on equity. These expectations may decline much more gradually than the actual ROE.

Question 7

A.

Company	Price	BV/ Share	P/BV	Beta	Exp. Growth	Payout	ROE
Air & Water	$9.60	$8.48	1.13	1.65	10.50%	0.00%	4.72%
Allwaste	$5.40	$3.10	1.74	1.10	18.50%	0.00%	8.06%
Browning Ferris	$29.00	$11.50	2.52	1.25	11.00%	46.90%	12.61%
Chemical Waste	$9.40	$3.75	2.51	1.15	2.50%	33.33%	12.00%
Groundwater	$15.00	$14.45	1.04	1.00	3.00%	0.00%	4.50%
Intern'l Tech.	$3.30	$3.35	0.99	1.10	11.00%	0.00%	4.78%
Ionics Inc.	$48.00	$31.00	1.55	1.00	14.50%	0.00%	7.10%
Laidlaw Inc.	$6.30	$5.85	1.08	1.15	8.50%	30.00%	6.84%
OHM Corp.	$16.00	$5.65	2.83	1.15	9.50%	0.00%	10.62%
Rollins	$5.10	$3.65	1.40	1.30	1.00%	0.00%	1.37%
Safety-Kleen	$14.00	$9.25	1.51	1.15	6.50%	45.00%	8.65%

Average   1.66   1.18   8.77% 14.11%   7.39%

Dividend Payout = DPS/EPS

ROE = EPS/ BV of Equity

The average price/book value ratio of these firms is 1.66, based on the following:

(1) These firms have, on average, a lower growth rate than the firm being valued.

(2) The firm being valued has more free cash flows available for paying dividends than the average firm in the sector.

(3) The firm is unlevered. It should therefore have a lower beta.

B. What subjective adjustments would you make to the price/book value ratio for this firm and why?

On all three counts, a higher price/book value ratio should be used for this company.

C. P/BV = - 0.105 + 0.51 Beta - 4.24 Growth - 1.76 Payout + 24.15 ROE

R^2= 0.84

The coefficients in this regression measure the change in P/BV ratio that would occur for a unit change in these variables. (Because of the multicollinearity, be cautious of reading too much into these coefficients.)

For the firm being valued,

Beta = 1.18/(1 + (1 - 0.4)(.20)) = 1.05 (The firm has no debt. Hence, the unlevered beta.)

Expected Growth Rate = 25%

Payout Ratio = ($3.50 - $2.50)/$3.50 = 0.2857

ROE = $3.50/20 = 17.50%

P/BV = -0.105 + 0.51 (1.05) - 4.24 (.25) -1.76 (0.2857) + 24.15 (.175)

= 3.09

Question 8

A. The R squared of the regression measures the goodness of fit of the regression. A high R squared would provide the user with more comfort with the predictions from using the regression.

B. P/BV = 0.88 + 0.82 (0.2857) + 7.79 (.25) - 0.41 (1.05) + 13.81 (.175)
     = 5.05

This regression uses the information in the entire cross-section, and hence might capture more of the differences across firms in other industries.

PRICE/SALES MULTIPLES

Question 1
A. True. Revenues cannot be negative.

B. False. It depends upon the profit margins of a firm's particular business.

C. False. The expected growth may go up to offset the lost profit margins.

D. True.

E. False. It depends upon the prices you pay for the high profit margins.

Question 2
A.   Dividend Payout Ratio = $1.12/$2.45 = 0.4571

Expected Growth Rate = 6%

Cost of Equity = 7% + 0.9 (5.5%) = 11.95%

Profit Margin = 2.45/122 = 2%

P/S Ratio = .02 * 0.4571 * (1.06)/(.1195 - .06) = 0.16288

Price Based on this Multiple = 0.16288 * 122 = $19.87

B.   P/S Ratio Needed for a Price of $34 = $34/122 = 0.2787

Profit Margin Needed for this P/S Ratio

= 0.2787 * (.1195 - .06)/(0.4571 * 1.06)

= 0.0342 or 3.42%

Question 3
A. These are the two companies with high expected growth rates. These high growth rates may explain the high P/S ratios. In addition, the Bombay company has the highest profit margin of the group.

B.

Correlation between P/S ratio and profit margin =	0.8840
Correlation between P/S ratio and expected growth =	0.7694
Correlation between P/S ratio and beta =	0.2754
Correlation between P/S ratio and payout =	-0.4390

C. One measure that might work is the ratio of Price/Sales (P/S) ratio to profit margin. On this basis, Bradlee's which has a P/S ratio of 0.09 and a profit margin of 1.04%, Caldor and Sears are most likely to be undervalued, whereas the Bombay company with P/S-Margin ratio of 0.56 is most likely to be overvalued.

Company	Price	Sales	P/S Ratio	Profit Margin	Exp. Growth	Beta	P/S-Margin
Bombay Co.	$38	$9.70	3.92	7.01%	29.00%	1.45	0.559
Bradlees	15	168.6	0.09	1.04%	12.00%	1.15	0.086
Caldor	32	147.45	0.22	1.83%	12.50%	1.55	0.119
Consol. Store	21	23	0.91	4.13%	26.50%	1.35	0.221
Dayton Hudson	73	272.9	0.27	1.70%	12.50%	1.3	0.157
Federated	22	58.9	0.37	2.38%	10.00%	1.45	0.157
Kmart	23	101.45	0.23	1.72%	11.50%	1.3	0.131
Nordstrom	36	43.85	0.82	3.65%	11.50%	1.45	0.225
Penney	54	81.05	0.67	4.32%	10.50%	1.1	0.154
Sears	57	150	0.38	3.03%	11.00%	1.35	0.125
Tiffany's	32	35.65	0.9	4.21%	10.50%	1.5	0.213
Wal-Mart	30	29.35	1.02	3.58%	18.50%	1.3	0.286
Woolworth	23	74.15	0.31	1.82%	13.00%	1.25	0.17

Alternatively, a regression of P/S ratios against the fundamental variables could have been run and estimated P/S ratios can be obtained.

Question 4

A.

Profit Margin = 221/8298 = 2.66%

$$PS = 0.0266 * \left[\frac{0.31*(1.135)*\left(1 - \frac{(1.135)^5}{(1.13325)^5}\right)}{(.13325 - .135)} + \frac{0.60*(1.135)^5*(1.06)}{(.13325-.06)(1.13325)^5} \right]$$

= 0.275

B. P/S ratio for Stable Growth Firm with Same Margin

= 0.0266 * 0.6 * 1.06/(.13325 - .06) = 0.231

P/S ratio attributable to High Growth = 0.275 - 0.231 = 0.044

Question 5

A.

$$PS = 0.1784 * \left[\frac{0.45 * (1.11) * \left(1 - \frac{(1.11)^5}{(1.125)^5}\right)}{(.125 - .11)} + \frac{0.60 * (1.11)^5 * (1.06)}{(.125-.06)(1.125)^5} \right]$$

= 2.02

B. New Margin = 100/700 = 14.29%

Old Growth Rate

= Old Profit Margin * Sales/Book Value * (1 - Payout ratio)

= .1784 * Sales/Book Value * (1 - 0.45) = 11%

Sales/Book Value = 1.12

New Growth Rate (for high growth period)

= .1429 * 1.12 * (1 - 0.45) = 8.81%

Price / Sales Ratio

$$= 0.1429 * \left[\frac{0.45 * (1.0881) * \left(1 - \frac{(1.0881)^5}{(1.125)^5} \right)}{(.125 - .0881)} + \frac{0.60 * (1.0881)^5 * (1.06)}{(.125 - .06)(1.125)^5} \right]$$

$$= 1.47$$

Question 6

A. McDonald's

	Next 10 years	After year 10
Payout Ratio	20.00%	65.00%
Sales/Book Value	1.20	1.20
Expected Growth Rate	14.03%	6.00%
Cost of Equity	12.775%	12.775%
Profit Margin	14.61%	14.61%

Expected Growth Rate = (1 - Payout Ratio) * Profit Margin * Sales/BV

$$= (1 - 0.2) * .1461 * 1.2 = 14.03\%$$

P/S Ratio = 1.97

Sales Per Share = 1.2 * 19 = $22.80

Price Per Share = 1.97 * ($22.80) = $44.93

Wendy's

	Next 10 Years	After Year 10
Payout Ratio	32.00%	65.00%
Sales/Book Value	2.00	2.00
Expected Growth	8.30%	6.00%
Cost of Equity	12.775%	12.775%
Profit Margin	6.10%	6.10%

P/S Ratio =	0.5711755
Price Per Share =	$8.00

B. If McDonald's sales/book value ratio remains unchanged and the profit margin drops to 6.10%:

	Next 10 Years	After Year 10
Payout Ratio	20.00%	65.00%
Sales/Book Value	1.20	1.20
Expected Growth Rate	5.86%	6.00%
Cost of Equity	12.775%	12.775%
Profit Margin	6.10%	6.10%

P/S Ratio =	0.41691165
Price Per Share =	$9.51

C. Value of McDonald's with its Current Profit Margin = $44.93
Value of McDonald's with Wendy's Profit Margin = $ 9.51
Difference in Value Per Share = $35.42
Value of Brand Name = $35.42 * Number of Shares Outstanding =
$$= 35.42 * (7.425/(19 * 1.2)) = \$11.54 \text{ Billion}$$

Question 7

A.

	Next 10 Years	*After Year 10*
Payout Ratio	33.00%	60.00%
Sales/Book Value	2.50	2.50
Expected Growth Rate	16.75%	6.00%

Cost of Equity	14.15%	12.50%
Profit Margin	10.00%	10.00%

P/S Ratio = 1.59991143

Price per share = $39.00

B.

	Next 10 Years	After Year 10
Payout Ratio	33.00%	60.00%
Sales/Book Value	3.00	3.00
Expected Growth Rate	16.08%	6.00%
Cost of Equity	14.15%	12.50%
Profit Margin	8.00%	8.00%

P/S Ratio = 1.21549194

Price Per Share = $35.55

C. The status quo strategy is best, since it leads to a higher price per share.

D. Sales would have to drop 20%. (Sales/book value ratio would have to be 2.40 for the two strategies to be equivalent.)

Question 8

A. No. One would explain its high price to sales ratio by pointing to the combination of a high profit margin and a moderate growth rate.

B. P/S = -0.79 + 11.50 Profit Margin + 0.60 Payout + 1.50 Growth + 0.51 Beta

Walgreen's predicted P/S ratio would be -

P/S = -0.79 + 11.50 (0.027) + 0.60 (.31) + 1.50 (.135) + 0.51 (1.15) = 0.4955

The small number of observations in this regression is of concerns, as are the signs on the coefficients for the variables. To the extent that the regression assumes that the relationship between P/S ratios and the fundamentals will not change, shifts in these relationships would also be cause for concern.

C. P/S = -0.79 + 11.50 (0.06) + 0.60 (0) + 1.50 (.20) + 0.51 (0.93) = 0.67
(The average beta for the industry was used, since this firm will have the same debt ratio as the average firm.)

Question 9
A. The coefficients on this regression measure both the direction and the magnitude of the relationship between P/S ratios and independent variables. My concerns would be the same as for the peer group regression.

B.

Company	P/S Ratio	Profit Margin	Payout	Exp. Growth	Beta	Predicted P/S
Arbor Drugs	0.42	3.40%	18%	14.00%	1.05	0.39904
Big B Inc.	0.30	1.90%	14%	23.50%	0.70	0.48704
Drug Emporium	0.10	0.60%	0%	27.50%	0.90	0.28121
Fay's Inc.	0.15	1.30%	37%	11.50%	0.90	0.34188
Genovese	0.18	1.70%	26%	10.50%	0.80	0.37292

Longs Drug	0.30	2.00%	46%	6.00%	0.90	0.38680
Perry Drugs	0.12	1.30%	0%	12.50%	1.10	0.14108
Rite Aid	0.33	3.20%	37%	10.50%	0.90	0.48487
Walgreen	0.60	2.70%	31%	13.50%	1.15	0.33992

These predictions use the information in the entire cross-section, and should be more reliable.

C. P/S   = 0.42 + 0.33 * 0 + 0.73 * 0.20 - 0.43 * 0.93 + 7.91 * 0.06

        = 0.64

The values in this regression are the values of the private firm being valued.

Market Value of Equity   = Revenues * Price/Sales Ratio

                = 250 * 0.64 = $160 million

MANAGEMENT DECISIONS, CORPORATE STRATEGY AND FIRM VALUE

Question 1

A. Price up

B. Impossible to tell. Some of the value that you pay for growth includes a premium for future positive NPV projects.

C. Price down

D. Price down. This is the equivalent of taking a negative NPV project.

E. No effect. Investing in T. Bonds is a zero NPV decision. They are assumed to be fairly priced.

Question 2

A. False. It may increase or it may decrease.

B. False.

C. True. Though it provides other benefits, the tax benefits dominate.

D. True. It is less risky and it provides a tax benefit.

E. False. The value of the firm is maximized.

(The value of equity per share is maximized.)

F. True.

Question 3

A. Cost of Equity = 7.25% + 1.85 (5.5%) = 17.425%

Value From Asset in Place   = EPS/ Cost of Equity
                            = $1.36/.17425 = $ 7.80

Total Value

= Value From Assets in Place + Value of Future Growth opportunities

= $7.80 + Value of Future Growth Opportunities = $39

Value of Growth Opportunities = $39 - $7.80 = $31.20
To calculate the value of assets in place, assume 100% payout and growth of zero.

B. No. The value of Broderbund owes a great deal to the expected positive NPV of future projects. Hence, when Broderbund takes on a positive NPV project, it may be in line with market expectations and not affect the price.

C. Yes. Here the price will drop.

Question 4
A. Value of Novell Prior to Acquisition Announcement
    = 308 million * $23.75 = $7.315 Billion

B. Value of Novell After the Acquisition Announcement
    = 308 * 20 = $6.160 Billion
Drop in Value of Novell
    = $7.315 Billion - $6.160 Billion = $1.155 Billion
If the entire drop is attributed to the decision to buy WordPerfect, the Value assigned to WordPerfect
    = $1.4 Billion - $1.155 Billion = $245 million

C. Given the size of the drop in market value, it seems likely that market participants are reacting not only to Novell's acquisition of WordPerfect, but also to the implicit message sent by that action on Novell's own projects, i.e., that it does not have very many. It may also reflect the trepidation that market participants feel about Novell's plans to grow by acquiring other firms.

Question 5

A. Expected Growth Rate = b (ROE) = 0.6 * 0.08 = 0.048 or 4.8%

Cost of Equity = 7.25% + 1.15 * 5.5% =13.575%

P/BV Ratio Based Upon 1993 levels

= (ROE -g)/(r-g) = (.08 - .048)/(.13575 - .048) = 0.36

B. If the firm improves its return on equity to 12%:

New Growth Rate = 0.6 * .12 = 0.072

P/BV Ratio = (.12 - .072)/(.13575 - .072) = 0.75

C. Yes. Taking on riskier projects would have pushed up the beta of the firm, reducing the benefit of the higher ROE.

Question 6

A. $$\frac{Price}{Earnings} = \frac{1}{0.136} + \left(\frac{0.135 - 0.136}{0.14 * 0.136} * \frac{1000}{540}\right) = 7.26$$

B. $$\frac{Price}{Earnings} = \frac{1}{0.136} + \left(\frac{0.16 - 0.136}{0.14 * 0.136} * \frac{1000}{540}\right) = 9.69$$

Question 7

A. Cost of Equity = 7% + 0.9 * 5.5% = 11.95%

   E/(D+E) = (22.2 * 31)/(22.2 * 31 + 435)=0.613

   After-tax Cost of Debt = 8.25%(0.6) = 4.95%

   D/(D+E) = 1 - 0.613 = 0.387

   WACC = 0.613 (.1195) + 0.387 (.0495) = 9.24%

B. FCFF this Year

   = EBIT (1-t) - (Cap Ex - Depreciation) - Δ Working Capital

   = 130 (0.6) - (96 - 76) = $58 million

Value of the Firm = 58 (1.06)/(.0924 - .06) = $1898 million

Value of Equity = $1898 - $435 = $1463 million

C. Unlevered Beta = 0.9/(1 + 0.6 * (435/(22.2 * 31))) = 0.65

New Debt/Equity Ratio = 335/(31 * 22.2 + 100) = 0.425

New Levered Beta = 0.65 * (1 + 0.6 * .425) = 0.82

New Cost of Equity = 7% + 0.82 (5.5%) = 11.51%

New Equity Ratio = 0.70

New After-Tax Cost of Debt = 7.75% (0.6) = 4.65%

New Debt Ratio = 0.30

New WACC = (.70) (.1151) + (.30) (.0465) = 9.46%

New Firm Value = 58 (1.06)/(.0946 - .06) = $1775 million

New Equity Value = $1775 - $335 = $1440 million

D. Unlevered Cost of Equity = 7% + 0.65 (5.5%) = 10.575%

Value of Firm at Old Debt Level

= 58 * 1.06/(.10575 - .06) + 0.4 (435) = $1518

Value of Firm at New Debt Level

= 58 * 1.06/(.10575 - .06) + 0.4 (335) = $1478

Question 8

E. Firms that exchange one security for another, and increase leverage in the process, increase their stock prices.

Question 9

A. Dividends are sticky. Companies do not change dividends very often.

E. When companies increase dividends, stock prices generally go up, and when they decrease dividends, stock prices generally go down.

Question 10

If a high growth firm announces that it is initiating dividends it can be viewed as a negative signal of future growth and projects. It can be tested by looking at firms that initiate dividends for the first time, to see if stock prices go down on the initiation. The empirical evidence actually suggests the contrary.

Question 11

A. *Long's Drug Store*

Cost of Equity = 7% + 0.9 (5.5%) = 11.95%

Return on Equity = $2.45/23.80 = 10.29%

Dividend Payout Ratio = 1.12/2.45 = 45.71%

Expected Growth Rate = b * ROE = (1 - 0.4571) * (.1029) = 5.59%

Value of Long's Based upon Existing Policy

= $1.12 (1.0559)/(.1195 - .0559) = $18.59

Walgreen

Cost of Equity = 7% + 1.15 * 5.5% = 13.325%

Return on Equity = $1.98/11.55 = 17.14%

Dividend Payout ratio = 0.60/1.98 = 30.30%

Expected Growth = (1 - .3030) (.1714) = 11.95%

Growth in Stable Growth Phase = (1 - .3030)(.13) = 9.06%

Value of Stock

$$
= \left[\frac{\$0.60 * (1.1195) * \left(1 - \dfrac{(1.1195)^5}{(1.13325)^5} \right)}{(.13325 - .1195)} + \frac{\$1.98 * (1.1195)^5 * (1.0906)*.3030}{(.13325-.0906)(1.13325)^5} \right]
$$

= $17.33

B. If Long's increases its payout ratio to 60%:

Expected Growth Rate = (1 - 0.6) (.1029) = 4.12%

Value of Long's Based Upon Higher Payout

= (2.45 * 0.6) (1.0411)/(.1195 - .0411) = $19.54

If Walgreen increases its payout ratio to 60%:

Expected Growth Rate in High Growth Period

= (1 - 0.6)(.1714) = 6.86%

Expected Growth in Stable Period = (1 - 0.6) (.13) = 5.2%

Value of Stock

$$= \left[\frac{\$1.98 * 0.6 * (1.0686) * \left(1 - \frac{(1.0686)^5}{(1.13325)^5}\right)}{(.13325 - .0686)} + \frac{\$1.98 * (1.0686)^5 * (1.052) * 0.60}{(.13325 - .052)(1.13325)^5} \right]$$

= $16.46

C. If Long's lowers its dividend payout ratio to 25%:

Expected Growth Rate = (1 - 0.25) (.1029) = 7.72%

Value Per Share   = (0.25 * $2.45)*(1.0772)/(.1195 - .0772)

= $15.60

If Walgreen lowers its payout ratio:

Value of Stock

$$= \left[\frac{\$1.98 * .25 * (1.1286) * \left(1 - \frac{(1.1286)^5}{(1.13325)^5}\right)}{(.13325 - .1286)} + \frac{\$1.98 * (1.1286)^5 * (1.0975) * .25}{(.13325 - .0975)(1.13325)^5} \right]$$

= $17.33

D. Companies which have good projects (high ROE) will generally gain by cutting back dividends, whereas companies with mediocre projects will gain by increasing them.

Question 12
A. & B.

	Without Restr.	With Restr.
ROA	6.91%	10.40%
Debt/Equity	159.41%	102.72%
Interest Rate	10.50%	10.50%
Dividend Payout	42.11%	21.05%
Payout After Year 5	14.85%	57.36%
Growth Rate-First 5 Years	4.08%	11.11%
Growth Rate-After Year 5	6.00%	6.00%
Beta	1.65	1.35
Cost Of Equity	16.08%	14.43%
Value	$2.69	$7.99

ROA Before = (Net Income + Interest (1-t))/(BV of Debt + BV of Equity)

Growth Rate-First 5 Years = (1 - Payout) (ROA + D/E (ROA - i (1-t))

Payout After 5 Years = 1 - g / (ROA + D/E (ROA - i (1-t))

Question 13
A.

	Current	1	2	3
Revenues	$450.00	$477.00	$505.62	$535.96
- COGS	$423.00	$443.61	$465.17	$487.72
- Deprec	$26.00	$27.56	$29.21	$30.97
= EBIT	$1.00	$5.83	$11.24	$17.27
- t (EBIT)	$0.40	$2.33	$4.49	$6.91

= EBIT(1-t)	$0.60	$3.50	$6.74	$10.36
- Cap Ex	$38.00	$40.28	$42.70	$45.26
+ Deprecn	$26.00	$27.56	$29.21	$30.97
- ∂ WC		$2.03	$2.15	$2.28
= FCFF		($11.25)	($8.89)	($6.21)

	4	5	Term Year
Revenues	$568.11	$602.20	$632.31
- COGS	$511.30	$535.96	$562.76
- Deprec	$32.82	$34.79	$36.53
= EBIT	$23.99	$31.45	$33.02
- t (EBIT)	$9.59	$12.58	$13.21
= EBIT(1-t)	$14.39	$18.87	$19.81
- Cap Ex	$47.97	$50.85	$36.53
+ Deprecn	$32.82	$34.79	$36.53
- ∂ WC	$2.41	$2.56	$2.26
FCFF	($3.17)	$0.25	$17.55
Term. Value		$300.95	
WACC =			11.02%
Present Value (@ 11.02%) =			$154.61
Value Per Share =			$6.18

B.

	Current	1	2	3
Revenues	$450.00	$477.00	$505.62	$535.96
- COGS	$423.00	$443.61	$469.22	$494.15

- Deprec	$26.00	$27.56	$29.21	$30.97
= EBIT	$1.00	$5.83	$7.19	$10.84
- t (EBIT)	$0.40	$2.33	$2.88	$4.34
= EBIT(1-t)	$0.60	$3.50	$4.31	$6.50
- Cap Ex	38	$40.28	$42.70	$45.26
+ Deprecn	$26.00	$27.56	$29.21	$30.97
- ∂ WC		$2.03	$2.15	$2.28
FCFF		($11.25)	($11.32)	($10.06)

Terminal Value

	4	5	Term Year
Revenues	$568.11	$602.20	$632.31
- COGS	$520.39	$548.00	$575.40
- Deprec	$32.82	$34.79	$36.53
= EBIT	$14.90	$19.40	$20.37
- t (EBIT)	$5.96	$7.76	$8.15
= EBIT(1-t)	$8.94	$11.64	$12.22
- Cap Ex	$47.97	$50.85	$36.53
+ Deprecn	$32.82	$34.79	$36.53
- ∂ WC	$2.41	$2.56	$2.26
= FCFF	($8.62)	($6.97)	$9.97
Terminal Value		$170.87	

WACC	11.02%
Present Value (@ 11.02%) =	$64.83
Value Per Share =	$2.59

CHAPTER 14 - SOLUTIONS
VALUATION FOR ACQUISITIONS/TAKEOVERS

Question 1

A. True. Synergy should increase the combined firm value.

B. False. Earnings volatility is generally firm specific. Even if it is not, investors can do this themselves at a much lower cost.

C. True. The combined firm will be safer making existing bonds more valuable.

D. True.

E. False.

Question 2

A. True. The value of control accrues from the changes that can be made in the firm after taking control of it.

B. False. Even if there is no imminent threat of a takeover, the probability of a takeover will keep the voting rights shares more valuable.

C. False. The evidence is mixed.

D. False. All stocks can go down in value.

E False. The empirical evidence does not support this statement, though some firms may do so.

Question 3

A. See below.

B. See below.

C. See below.

D. See below.

E.

	Grumman	Northrop	No synergy	With Synergy
Revenues	$3,281	$4,620	$7,901	$7,901
- COGS	$2,920	$4,043	$6,963	$6,795
- Deprecn	$74	$200	$274	$274
= EBIT	$287	$378	$664	$832
EBIT (1-t)	$187	$245	$432	$541
$-\partial$ WC	$16	$22	$38	$38
FCFF	$171	$223	$394	$503
Cost of Equity	12.50%	12.50%	12.50%	12.50%
Cost of Debt	5.53%	5.53%	5.53%	5.53%
WACC	11.38%	11.98%	11.73%	11.73%
Firm Value	$2,681	$3,199	$5,879	$7,479

Synergy Gain = $7479 - $5879 = $1,600

Note: Firm Value = $FCFF_1/(WACC - g)$

Question 4

A. & B.

	w/o Added Debt	With Added Debt
Revenues	$7,901	$7,901
- COGS	$6,795	$6,795
- Deprecn	$274	$274
= EBIT	$832	$832
EBIT (1-t)	$541	$541
$-\partial$ WC	$38	$38
FCFF	$503	$503

Beta	1.00	1.08
Cost of Equity	12.50%	12.92%
Cost of Debt	5.04%	5.20%
WACC	11.68%	11.37%

Firm Value	$7,540	$7,897

Beta with Added Debt = Unlevered Beta $(1 + (1 - t) (Debt/Equity))$
$$= 0.93 (1 + (1 - 0.4) (0.25)) = 1.08$$

C. The equity investors should gain the additional value of $357 million.

Question 5

A. , B., C., & D.:

	Novell	*WordPerfect*	*No synergy*	*w/ Synergy*
Revenues	$1500	$690		$2,232
COGS	$855	$518		$1,406
Depreciation	$53	$29		$83
EBIT	$593	$144		$743
EBIT (1-t)	$385	$93		$483
- Cap Expenditure	$94	$46		$143
+ Depreciation	$53	$29		$83
- ∂ Working Capital	$120	$27		$147
FCFF	$224	$49		$276

Cost of Equity (Initial)	14.98%	13.88%		14.85%
Cost of Equity (Stable)	13.05%	13.05%		13.05%
Value of firm	$12,059	$1,554	$13,613	$14,377

The cost of equity is also the weighted average cost of capital because neither firm has any debt. The weights are based upon the estimated values.

(The free cash flow to the firm under synergy in year 1 is greater than the sum of the FCFF of the two individual firms because of the higher growth rate in cash flows. All the estimated numbers under synergy are based upon the new expected growth rate which is 24%.)

E. Value of Synergy = 14377 - 13613 = $764 million

Maximum Price for Wordperfect= 1554 + 764 = $2318 million

Question 6

A. Tax Savings Next Year = $2 Billion * 0.4 = $800 million

PV of Tax Savings = 800/1.12 = $714 million

B. PV of Tax Savings = $200 (PVA, 12%, 4 years) = $607.47 million

Question 7

A. , B. & C.

	PMT Corporation	*Peer Group*	*Best Managed*
Return On Assets	8.00%	12.00%	18.00%
Dividend Payout Ratio	50.00%	30.00%	20.00%
Debt Equity Ratio	10.00%	50.00%	50.00%
Interest Rate on Debt	7.50%	8.00%	8.00%
Beta	1.06	1.30	1.30
Growth Rate-First 5 Years	4.18%	10.92%	19.68%
Payout Ratio after Year 5	28.14%	61.54%	75.61%
Growth Rate After Year 5	6.00%	6.00%	6.00%

Cost of Equity	12.83%	14.15%	14.15%

Value of Equity Per Share	$12.65	$25.18	$41.94

Growth Rate-First 5 years = (1 - Payout) (ROA + D/E (ROA - i (1-t))

Payout After 5 Years = 1 - g / (ROA + D/E (ROA - i (1-t))

Question 8

A.

	1	2	3
Revenues	$1,100,000	$1,210,000	$1,331,000
- Expenses	$440,000	$484,000	$532,400
- Depreciation	$100,000	$110,000	$121,000
= EBIT	$560,000	$616,000	$677,600
- Interest Exp.	$360,000	$324,000	$288,000
= Taxable Income	$200,000	$292,000	$389,600
- Tax	$80,000	$116,800	$155,840
= Net Income	$120,000	$175,200	$233,760
+ Deprec'n	$100,000	$110,000	$121,000
- Cap. Exp	$120,000	$132,000	$145,200
- ∂ WC	$20,000	$22,000	$24,200
- Principal Repaid	$300,000	$300,000	$300,000
= FCFE	($220,000)	($168,800)	($114,640)
+ Int (1-t)	$216,000	$194,400	$172,800
+ Princ. Repaid	$300,000	$300,000	$300,000
= FCFF	$296,000	$325,600	$358,160

	4	5	Term. Year
Revenues	$1,464,100	$1,610,510	$1,707,141
- Expenses	$585,640	$644,204	$682,856
- Depreciation	$133,100	$146,410	$155,195
= EBIT	$745,360	$819,896	$869,090
- Interest Exp.	$252,000	$216,000	$180,000
= Taxable Income	$493,360	$603,896	$689,090
- Tax	$197,344	$241,558	$275,636
= Net Income	$296,016	$362,338	$413,454
+ Deprec'n	$133,100	$146,410	$155,195
- Cap. Exp	$159,720	$175,692	$186,234
- ∂ WC	$26,620	$29,282	$19,326
- Principal Repaid	$300,000	$300,000	$0
= FCFE	($57,224)	$3,774	$363,089
+ Int (1-t)	$151,200	$129,600	$108,000
+ Princ. Repaid	$300,000	$300,000	$0
= FCFF	$393,976	$433,374	$471,089

B.

	1	2	3
Equity	1,000,000	1,120,000	1,295,200
Debt	3,000,000	2,700,000	2,400,000
D/E Ratio	3.00	2.41	1.85
Beta	2.58	2.25	1.95
Cost of Equity	24.90%	23.11%	21.41%
Cumulated COE	1.249	1.538	1.867
WACC	11.625%	11.864%	12.182%
Cum WACC	1.116	1.249	1.401

	4	5	6
Equity	1,528,960	1,824,976	2,187,314
Debt	2,100,000	1,800,000	1,500,000
D/E Ratio	1.37	0.99	0.69
Beta	1.68	1.47	1.30
Cost of Equity	19.95%	18.78%	17.86%
Cumulated COE	2.239	2.660	3.135
WACC	12.574%	13.028%	13.525%
Cum WACC	1.577	1.782	2.023

Cost of Equity in Year 2

$\qquad$ = Cost of Equity in Year 1 - (Beta$_2$ - Beta$_1$) * 5.5%

$\qquad$ = 24.90% - (2.58 - 2.25) * 5.5% = 23.11%

C. Terminal Value of Firm = $363,089/(.1786-.06) = $3,060,662

Terminal Value of Firm = Terminal Value of Equity + Outstanding Debt

= 3,060,662 + 1,500,000 = 4,560,662

D. PV to Equity Investors

= -220,000/1.249 -168800/(1.249)(1.2311) - 114640/

(1.2490)(1.2311)(1.2141) - 57224/(1.2490) (1.2311)(1.2141) (1.1995)

+ (3774 + 3060662)/(1.2490) (1.2311)(1.2141) (1.1995)(1.1878)

= $779220 < 1,000,000

Deal does not make sense from the viewpoint of equity investors.

PV to firm = Discount FCFF at WACC = 3,833,357 < 4,000,000

Overall, deal does not make sense.

CHAPTER 15 - SOLUTIONS

OPTION PRICING THEORY

Question 1

A. False. The reverse is true.

B. True. Higher variance increases option value.

C. True. Otherwise, arbitrage will be possible.

D. False. Put-call parity can cut both ways.

E. True. Dividends reduce the stock price.

F. True.

G. False. Some deep-in-the-money put options will be exercised early.

H. True. The time premium decreases.

I. True. The value of early exercise is more likely to overwhelm the time premium.

J. False. It is the variance that matters, not the beta.

Question 2

A.

At t=1,

if the stock price = $70	*if the stock price = $35*
Delta = 0.80	Delta = 0.00
Borrowing = $36.03	Borrowing = $0.00
Option Value = $19.96	Option Value = $0.00

At t=0.

Delta = 0.5704

Borrowing = $17.99

Option Value = $10.53

$$\text{Value of the Call (K=60, t=2)} = \$10.53$$

B.

At t=1,

if the stock price = $70	if the stock price=$35
Delta = -0.20	Delta = -1.00
Borrowing = -$18.02	Borrowing = -$54.05
Option Value = $4.02	Option Value = $19.05

At t=0,

Delta = -0.4296

Borrowing = $30.72

Option Value = $9.23

$$\text{Value of the Put (K=60, t=2)} = \$9.23$$

C. At t=0, the call can be replicated by borrowing $17.99 and buying 0.57 shares of stock.

At t=1, the call can be replicated by borrowing $36.04 and buying 0.8 shares of stock if the stock price goes to $70, and by doing nothing if the stock price goes to $35.

D. At t=0, the put can be replicated by selling short 0.43 shares of stock and lending $30.71.

At t=1, the put can be replicated by selling short 0.2 shares of stock and lending $18.02 if the stock price goes to $70 and by selling short one share of stock and lending $54.05 if the stock price goes to $35.

Question 3

A. The values of the option parameters are as follows:

S = $83

K = $85

t = 0.25

r = 3.80%

Variance = 0.09

Value of call = $4.42

B. To replicate this call, you would have to:

Buy 0.4919 Shares of Stock (this is N(d1) from the model)

and

Borrow K e^{-rt} N(d2) = 85 exp$^{-(0.038)(0.25)}$ (0.4324) = $36.40

C. At an implied variance of 0.075, the call has a value of approximately $4.00 (the market price).

Implied Standard Deviation = $\sqrt{0.075}$ = 0.2739

D.

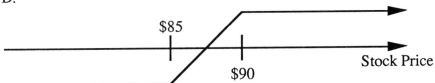

E.

Value of Three-month Put = C - S + Ke^{-rt} = $4.42 - $83 + 85 exp$^{-(0.038)(0.25)}$ = $5.62

Question 4

A.   S = $28.75

K = $30

t = 0.25

r = 3.60%

$\sigma^2 = 0.04$

PV of Expected Dividends $= \$0.28/(1.036)^{2/12} = \$0.28$

Value of Call $= \$0.64$

B. The payment of a dividend reduces the expected stock price, and hence reduces the value of calls and increases the value of puts.

Question 5

A. First value the three-month call, as above:

Value of Call $= \$0.64$

Then, value a call to the first (and only) dividend payment,

$S = \$28.75$

$K = \$30$

$t = 2/12$

$r = 3.60\%$

$\sigma^2 = 0.04$

$y = 0$ (since it assumes exercise before the dividend payment)

Value of Call $= \$0.51$

Since the value of the three-month call is higher, there is no anticipated exercise.

B. If the dividend payment is large enough, it may pay to exercise the call just before the ex-dividend day (before the stock price drops) rather than wait until expiration. This early exercise is more likely for call options:

(a) the larger the dividend on the stock, and

(b) the closer the option is to expiration.

Question 6

A. You would need to borrow Ke^{-rt} N(d2) = 90 exp$^{(-0.04)(0.25)}$ (0.4500) = $40.10

B. You would need to buy 0.575 shares of stock.

Question 7

A.   S= $4.00

$K = $4.25

$r = 5\%$

$t = 1$

Variance = 0.36

Value of Warrant = $0.93

B. Adjusted Stock Price = (Stock Price * Number of Shares Outstanding) + (Warrant price * Number of Warrants Outstanding)/(Number of Shares+Number of Warrants)

      = ($4.00 * 11,000,000 + $0.93 * 550,000)/(11,550,000) = $3.85

(To avoid the circular reasoning problem, the price from the no-dilution case is used.)

Adjusted Exercise Price = $4.25

$r = 5\%$

$t = 1$

Variance = 0.36

Value of Warrant = $0.80

(If you are using a spreadsheet with iterations turned on, and are feeding the option prices back to calculate the adjusted stock price, the value of the warrants is still $0.80.)

C. Dilution increases the number of shares outstanding. For any given value of equity, each share is worth less.

Question 8

A. $S = 250$

$K = 275$

$t = 5$

$r = 5\%$

$\sigma^2 = (0.15)^2$

$y = 0.03$

Value of call = $29.09

B. Value of put with same parameters = $28.09

C.

(1) The variance will be unchanged for the life of the option. This is likely to be violated because stock price variances do change substantially over time.

(2) There will be no early exercise. This is reasonable and is unlikely to be violated.

(3) Any deviations from the option value will be arbitraged away. While there are plenty of arbitrageurs eager to exploit deviations from true value, arbitraging an index is clearly more difficult to do than arbitraging an individual stock.

Question 9

New Security   = AT & T stock - Call (K=60) + Put (K=45)

= $50 - $2.35 + $3.55 = $51.20

The call with a strike price of $60 is sold, eliminating upside potential above $60.

The put with a strike price of $45 is bought, providing downside protection.

CHAPTER 16 - SOLUTIONS
APPLICATIONS OF OPTION PRICING THEORY TO VALUATION

Question 1

A. True. Equity investors cannot lose more than their equity investment.

B. False. They can make equity more valuable, not the firm.

C. True. It transfers wealth to the bondholders.

D. True. This is the equivalent of the life of the option.

E. True. There is a transfer of wealth to bondholders.

Question 2

A. Value of the firm = 40 (1-0.4)/(.10-.05) = $480 million

B. $\quad$ S = $480

$\quad$ K = $500

$\quad$ t = 5 years

$\quad$ r = 5%

$\quad$ σ=0.125

Note: Since the dividends are paid to the stockholders, and we are valuing equity, it is not shown as a dividend yield.

Value of Call (Equity) = $106.39

C. Value of Debt = $480 - $106.39 = $373.61 million

Appropriate Interest Rate = $(500/373.61)^{(1/5)}$ - 1 = 6.00%

Question 3

A. Firm Value

$$= \frac{\$850*0.6*(1.20)*\left(1-\frac{(1.20)^5}{(1.10)^5}\right)}{.10-.05} + \frac{\$850*0.6*1.2^5*1.05}{(.10-.05)(1.10)^5} = \$19,883$$

B. Standard Deviation of Firm

$= [(0.67)^2(0.35)^2 + (0.33)^2 (0.15)^2 + 2 (0.67)(0.33) (.5) (.35) (.15)$

$= 0.2619$

S = 19,883.21	r=5%
K = FV of Debt = 10,000	Variance = 0.2619^2 = 0.0686
t = Average Duration of Debt = 3	Dividend Yield = 0
d1 = 2.07	N(d1) = 0.9808
d2 = 1.62	N(d2) = 0.9472

Value of Call (Equity) = $11,350

C. Market Value of Equity = $12,200

Implied Variance = 0.25

Implied Standard Deviation = 0.5

D. Market Value of Debt = $8,534

Question 4

A. PV of Inflows $= 400,000 * 0.85 * (1 - 1.04^{25}/1.07^{25})/(.07 - .04)$

$\qquad = \$5,766,648$

PV of Outflows

$\qquad = -3,000,000 - 400,000 * 0.40 * (1 - 1.03^{25}/1.07^{25})/(.07 - .03)$

$\qquad = 5,456,892$

NPV = 5,766,648 - 5,456,892 = $309,755

B.   S = 5,766,648

K = 5,456,892

t = 25

r = 7%

σ = 0.25

y = 1/25 = 4%

Value of the Call Option = $1,639,438

C. The latter considers the option characteristics of owning the mine, i.e., that copper prices may go up, and is higher.

Question 5

Current Value of Developed Reserve

= 10,000,000 * ($20 - $6) = $140,000,000

Exercise Price = Cost of Developing Reserve = $120,000,000

t = 20 years

r = 7%

σ = 20%

y = 4%

Value of Call (Natural Resource Reserve) = $37,360,435

Question 6

A. NPV of Project = $250 - $200 = $50 million

B. The option has the following characteristics:

S = 250

K =200

r = 8%

t = 5

Variance = 0.04

Dividend Yield = 12.5/250 = 5%

Value of Call (Project Rights) = $68.68

C. The latter captures the value of delaying the project. The difference between the two values will increase as the variance in the project cash flows increases.

Question 7

A.   S = PV of Cash Inflows on Project = 250

       K = Cost of Taking Project = 500

       t = 10 years

       r = 6%

       σ = 0.6

       y = 10/250 = 4%

Value of Call (Product Patent) = $95 million

B. It is an increasing function of the variance in project cash flows. This analysis suggests that the rights to products in technologically volatile areas are likely to be worth a great deal, even though the products may not be viable now.

Question 8

A. False. It is the uncertainty that makes the project valuable.

B. True. Without this protection, there would be no option.

C. False. The value of these projects can be accounted for in the growth rate.

D. False. It may pay to wait for the project to become more valuable.

E. True.

INDEX